To the seamen of the Western Isles, especially those who, in peace and war, saved other lives at the risk of their own.

SURPRISE ISLAND

"Rich colourful reminiscences...funny tales, strange episodes, tragedies and adventures...A delightful book" Gerry Davis in the T.V. programme "Cover to Cover".

THE HUB OF MY UNIVERSE

"...emotions and real-life conflicts a-plenty...I for one hope he will write more." Trevor Royle in the "Glasgow Herald".

"But most memorable of all are the intense, unforgettable impressions of a Stornoway boy — in his infancy, at school, as a journalistic apprentice and as the official scribe of some fascinating court cases." Cuthbert Graham in the "Press & Journal".

"Altogether a wise and unpretentious book...We can all learn from it." Iain Crichton Smith in the "Scotsman".

HIGHLAND VILLAGES

"...a village is not a fossilized group of buildings...but a living community with problems, aspirations and prejudices, arising from the past and influencing the future."

THEIR CHILDREN WILL SEE
and other stories

"They have a unique tone of voice.. what comes over is controlled and elegiac passion." Douglas Gifford in "Books in Scotland".

"...there is a feeling of truth...an uneasy feeling because it is not the kind of truth we are used to," Naomi Mitchison in "Books and Bookmen."

THE GAELIC VIKINGS

James Shaw Grant

Humour   Adventure   Mystery
Pirates Poltergeists Heroes

Published by James Thin Ltd, 53-59 South Bridge, Edinburgh, in collaboration with the author, James Shaw Grant, Ardgrianach, Inshes, Inverness. IV1 2BQ.

ISBN 0 9508371 2 1

Printed in the Scottish Highlands by Nevisprint Limited, Fort William.

Contents

	page
Law-abiding Anarchists	1
Nelson's Stick and Charlie's Ring	5
Conversation in a Butcher's Shop	9
The "King" was Poeno's Friend	13
Fire Upon the Rascals!	17
Before Kon-tiki	21
The Golden Ring of Palmyra	25
Toy and Tallahassee	29
A "Black" Santa Claus	33
Mac an t-Srònaich was a "Fantom"	36
Two Mysteries Remain	40
A Corsair from the Throat of Tunis	44
Why Rory Shot the Sun	48
Spanish Coins in a Secret Drawer	52
The Cabin Boy's Story	55
Beeswax By the Creelful	57
Duel at Tong Sands	60
Who was Capt Delano?	63
Lightning Strikes Twice	66
Hannah Ceard and Catriona Glas	69
The Shop Assistants' Silver Stone	72
The Three Times of Tolsta	75
No Bicycles in the Bible	78
Neil Gunn and a Prayer Meeting	81
The Crazy Machismo of the Pubs	83
The Thunder is in Good Hands	86

The Tolsta Chaolais Poltergeist … … … … … … … … … … … 89

The Plane Made its Own Fog … … … … … … … … … … … 92

The Song of the Bernera Bachelors … … … … … … … … … … 95

Mens Sana in Corpore Sano … … … … … … … … … … … 98

They Danced at the Hens' Wedding … … … … … … … … … 101

Conversation Lozenges … … … … … … … … … … … … 104

Two Loves a Week … … … … … … … … … … … … … 107

Cut Price Justice … … … … … … … … … … … … … … 110

The Red Haired Poachers of Big Bull … … … … … … … … 113

Other Things to Think of … … … … … … … … … … … 116

The Night of the Black Iceberg … … … … … … … … … … 119

The Price of Admiralty … … … … … … … … … … … … 122

A Cry Across the Crofts … … … … … … … … … … … … 125

He Tried to Quieten the Night … … … … … … … … … … 128

Swedes at a Bernera Wedding … … … … … … … … … … 131

It was Greek to Them … … … … … … … … … … … … 134

Six Days and Nights at the Tiller … … … … … … … … … 138

A Lewisman's Twelve Pianos … … … … … … … … … … 142

Thirty Thousand DSM's … … … … … … … … … … … 145

Courage Beyond all Praise … … … … … … … … … … … 149

Three Lewismen — and Eighty … … … … … … … … … … 152

The Crew of the Rose of Shader … … … … … … … … … 156

Where Scroobie was King … … … … … … … … … … … 159

The Fish Spoke Gaelic … … … … … … … … … … … … 162

Lewis Prime Minister and London Prostitutes … … … … … … 165

Surprises Still in Store … … … … … … … … … … … … 168

Acknowledgements

Many people have contributed to the making of this book. As far as possible I have acknowledged borrowings in the text where they occur, but much of the information came to me long ago, from sources I have forgotten, and which can only be acknowledged in a very general way.

What began as an individual exercise of memory has become almost a communal enterprise, so many people have written to me, unsolicited, or in response to requests for help. When I mentioned *The Old Lewis Guard,* for instance, as a book I had seen in a shop window, as a child, but had never read, I received a complete photocopy from John MacKay Shaw, a Stornoway man, in Tallahassee, Florida.

I mention in several places that information has come to me from William Matheson and Donald Macdonald, in Edinburgh, but I have drawn on them so much as sources I feel a general acknowledgement is due as well.

Apart from material used in this book, readers have sent me interesting snippets of information about incidents described in the earlier books in the series, *The Hub of My Universe* and *Surprise Island.* Alick John Macrae, for instance, writes from his schoolhouse in North Kessock to tell me that all the old soldiers of Uig, who had daughters, called them Jean, after the wife of one of their officers, but the name is now out of fashion in Uig. While Roddie H. MacLeod, applying an accountant's mind to Mary Carn's fortune, tells me that, in modern money, it was in the region of £850,000. No wonder they broached a cask of Madeira when she died, and got gloriously drunk at the funeral!

In addition to those who provided information directly, I have to thank the Scottish Arts Council for a grant towards the cost of research into a number of matters, which will be dealt with in later volumes, if not used herein. I appreciate the SAC assistance particularly because any profit from the series, of which this is one, will go to an educational project in the Western Isles, so that, if the books are successful, as they look like being, the SAC grant will be rolled over, so to speak, to serve another purpose, in another place.

Above all, I wish to thank my wife, Cathie, who first persuaded me to write these books, and has contributed greatly to them as they have developed.

The *Journal* and other papers of James Morison, bosun's mate on the *Bounty* are now preserved in the Mitchell Library in Sydney, Australia. At the request of the Library authorities, I have deposited there a record of the oral tradition on which my claim that he was a Lewisman is based. In turn I am indebted to the Library for the opportunity of drawing on the Golden Cockerel edition of the *Journal* for some of the material in the early chapters of this book.

In a fit of perverse pedantry I have spelt the bosun's name with one "r" to emphasise the fact that he is a descendant of Mori, not of Morris. Morison himself favoured the double "r", as the great majority of Lewis Morrisons do, but many members of my mother's family made a fetish of using one "r", especially my auntie Jessie, to whom I am indebted for the information which led me to the mutineer's identity. A little gesture in her direction seems appropriate!

1
Law-Abiding Anarchists

When the film "Mutiny on the *Bounty*" came to Stornoway, with Charles Laughton as the notorious Capt Bligh, my aunt announced that she was going to see it. I was horrifed. Jessie was an elderly and very timid spinster. The brutality would sicken her.

"I want to see it," she persisted. "James Morison was a relative of ours."

That made it worse. James Morison, the bosun's mate, was the man who wielded the cat o' nine tails when Bligh ordered a flogging. I wondered what Jessie would think of her relative when she heard the lash and saw the blood spurt.

A few days later she announced that she had seen the film, adding triumphantly, "James Morison *is* a relative of ours. The family resemblance was unmistakable!"

Poor Jessie! She was a real innocent. The kindest creature on earth, but always blurting out the things the rest of the family discreetly avoided.

When I expostulated with her for foisting a mutineer on the family she added sweetly that we had a murderer as well. The most notorious murderer in Lewis history. Mac an t-Sronaich, the ogre of my childhood! The Yorkshire Ripper was gentle in comparison.

"My granny used to put out food for him" she said, telling me precisely where the house was, and which window the food was placed in.

I didn't take her seriously, and after a few perfunctory enquiries I dismissed the matter from my mind. Forty years later, nearly a quarter of a century after she was dead, I found that Jessie was right. On both counts! And on other things as well!

At the same time I discovered why I am writing this book — or rather the series of books of which this is one. I have no option! It is bedded in my genes. Three hundred years ago, almost precisely, my great-grandfather's great-grandfather's grandfather, John Morison of Bragar, sat down to write the first account of life in Lewis ever written by a native. Since then every direct ancestor on my mother's side of the family has been deeply involved in the affairs of the island — except one.

The renegade was John's son, Roderick, the celebrated Blind Harper of Dunvegan — An Clarsair Dall. He devoted his not inconsiderable talents as a bard to celebrating the aristocracy of Skye, instead of the ordinary people of egalitarian Lewis, as I am trying to do now. If anyone in Lewis is ordinary, that is!

The mutineer and the murderer, whose skeletons Jessie dragged from the

1

family cupboard, and the genial hobo, known as the Claw, whom she added for good measure, are merely high points, Himalayan peaks, in the human geography of an island of rugged individualists.

Many years ago I defined the Lewisman as a law-abiding anarchist. A man of peace (by and large) who still insists on going his own way, regardless. Who combines with uncompromising personal independence an unusually strong sense of family and community. Whose ebullient male machismo is tamed with surprising ease, sometimes by the church, sometimes by matrimony, but generally by old age.

Without being critical of the churches, or the wives, I prefer my fellow islanders (and myself!), not unregenerate, but certainly unsubdued.

It is misleading to encapsulate a whole community in an aphorism, as I have done; especially a community of individualists, but there is some truth in my definition, and it certainly fits snugly the career of James Morison who was condemned to death as a mutineer, pardoned because of his excellent record as a seaman, and restored to his post of gunner in the navy at the specific request of Admiral Sir Thomas Troubridge who wanted him on his flagship.

But was James Morison a Lewisman as Jessie claimed? His career is well documented in his own writings, which are preserved in the Mitchell Library in Sydney, Australia, and in numerous books about the mutiny by other people, but nowhere is Lewis mentioned. In fact for a hundred and ninety years he seems to have been regarded as a Londoner.

There is nothing intrinsically improbable in Jessie's story that there was a Lewisman on the *Bounty*. After all there was both a Shetlander and an Orcadian.

Peter Linkletter, the Shetlander, was one of those who went with Bligh after the mutiny, and took part in the great open boat voyage of 3623 miles from the Friendly Islands to Timor. He died in Batavia, no doubt as a result of his experience.

The history of George Stewart the Orcadian is even more eventful. He fell in love with a Tahitian princess, married her and had a daughter. When the navy caught up with the mutineers, he was imprisoned on HMS *Pandora,* in the little hut built on the deck which Morison dubbed "Pandora's box". He was drowned when the *Pandora* was wrecked. The first missionaries to Tahiti found that his princess had died of a broken heart, after their enforced separation, but the daughter was still alive, cared for by her Tahitian relatives.

Byron used the story for his long poem *The Island* but got his geography mixed, making the hero that impossible creature a Hebridean from Orkney:

> *"The fair-haired offspring of the Hebrides,*
> *Where roars the Pentland with its swirling seas".*

The odd thing is that, while the provenence of the Orcadian and the

Shetlander, has always been well-known (Byron's gaffe apart) the history of the Lewisman, the most considerable figure of the three, was completely lost sight of by the historians, and might have disappeared for ever if my auntie Jessie had not gone to the cinema to see Charles Laughton.

Fortunately, I asked Jessie's brothers whether they could confirm her story. Their replies meant nothing to me at the time but, in the event, they proved to be more significant than if they had been direct.

Willie, a doctor in Durham, who was romantically interested in everything Lewis and everything Gaelic, told me that, as a boy, he had frequently heard it said that one of his seafaring relatives, James Morison, had been "king of a South Sea Island". On the face of it, that is far removed from being bosun's mate on HMS *Bounty,* and a mutineer to boot, but I'll come back to it.

Roddie, a minister in Stornoway who had little interest in family gossip, replied to my query with a question of his own, "Where on earth did Jessie get that story?"

"She says she got it from Magaidh a' Chaiptein," I replied.

"That's different," he said. "Magaidh a' Chaiptein was in a position to know!"

I had no idea who Magaidh a' Chaiptein was, or why she was in a position to know, until — nearly forty years later — I picked up William Matheson's excellent book on The Blind Harper in the Gaelic Texts Society's series.

Matheson gives detailed genealogies of the descendants of the Harper's great-great-grandfather, John Morison, the thirteenth, and last, of the hereditary Breves, or lawmen, of Lewis, who died around 1600.

Oddly, for a lawman, John Morison was guilty of adultery, piracy and abduction. The adultery was committed with the wife of his chief, which was doubly indiscreet. The piracy involved the seizure of a Dutch ship laden with wine. The abduction followed, when he invited his arch enemy, Domhnull Cam Macaulay, aboard to share the spoils with him, got him drunk, and lashed him to the mast. Domhnull Cam escaped with a huge weight tied to his ankle which, according to tradition, was a showpiece at Dunvegan Castle for many years thereafter.

The Breve's misdeeds caught up with him when he met his end in a bloody brawl, in Inverkirkaig in Assynt. His henchmen tried to take his body home for burial but were stormbound on a little island off Lochinver, still known as the Breve's Island. There they gralloched him, when he began to stink, with the result that his intestines are buried in Sutherland, and the rest of him in Lewis.

The last of the Breves was clearly the representative of a society and polity in disarray, which makes a nonsense of the popular belief that the watershed for the Gaelic-speaking Highlanders came at Culloden.

When some order was restored in the area, and the Hebrides were effectively absorbed into the larger Scottish, and finally the United, Kingdom, the energies of the Breve's descendants flowed into other

3

channels. Two of them, who are also — and more obviously — descended from the Breve's arch enemy, Domhnull Cam Macaulay, are buried in Westminster Abbey: the only instance on record, so far as I know, of a father and son both being accorded that honour. The father, Zachary, was buried in the Abbey because of his work for the emancipation of the slaves. The son, Lord Macaulay, for his History of England, and for giving India a legal code for which his name is still revered.

Among the other motley descendants, listed by Matheson, of the ruffian whose burial straddled the Minch, I found, nine generations on, the name of Magaidh a' Chaiptein, and at once it became clear why she was "in a position to know" whether the bosun's mate on the *Bounty* was Lewisman or not.

2
Nelson's Stick and Charlie's Ring

I knew quite a bit about Magaidh a'Chaiptein when my uncle mentioned her although at the time, I did not know I knew.

Thinking back, as I write, fragments of overheard conversations, which bored me as a child, come welling up from the depths of memory. It is always difficult to know how much is memory and how much is imagination, when one dredges into the recesses like this, but it seems to me that the original print is less likely to be tainted if one was not interested in it at the time. When we are involved in what we are listening to, we tend to censor our impressions as we stow them away, while those which come unsought lie as they fell.

Maggie was a music teacher. She taught the piano to my mother and some of my aunts, including Jessie. It is probably in idle moments during these lessons that Jessie and Maggie wandered into family history. Mutual family history, as it happens. Both were related to the mutineer, although Maggie was not as closely related as Jessie.

My mother mentioned Magaidh a' Chaiptein to me more than once. Not because of James Morison and the *Bounty,* but to illustrate her own folly. She was fond of music, but one day, in the middle of a piano lesson, she decided that her hands were ugly. She didn't like the look of them on the keyboard, and never touched the piano again.

Her real enjoyment of music was delayed well into her forties when we got our first radio, and our first gramophone: a wheezy, scratchy instrument with steel needles, which had generally to be rewound half way through a record, reducing a basically discordant reproduction to absolute incoherence. But how we loved it, and how we marvelled!

Because of her own experience, my mother was determined that I should learn to play the piano, and purchased, at considerable sacrifice, an expensive instrument on which I could be taught. Unfortunately, I had no ear for music, and at the same time, received from an uncle a gift of boxing gloves. The boxing gloves won. Hands down! Or rather, hands up! Not that I ever boxed with them in any meaningful way but I, and my particular pal at that time, Charlie Macarthur, son of the Leurbost minister, liked to think we were Jack Dempsey — both of us simultaneously! — and put on a nightly performance in our back garden which was closer to play-acting than fisticuffs.

I understood from my mother that Magaidh a' Chaiptein was, in the jargon of the time, a decayed gentlewoman. It was "beneath her station" to be a teacher of music. I also gathered the impression that her brother had something to do with the decline in the family fortunes. He died ten years before I was born, but he still reverberates in my memory because of his nickname — Killiecrankie!

The link with the *Bounty* was provided by Maggie's grand-mother, Lilias Morison, who was a hundred years old when she died in 1864. By that time Maggie was 28. The 1851 census for Stornoway shows that when Lilias was a widow, living alone, her son and her grandchildren lived just a few doors away. Maggie was then a schoolgirl of 16. It would be surprising if there was not considerable commerce between Maggie and her grandmother, and it would be equally surprising if, on her visits, they did not talk about family matters. Lilias certainly had a lot to talk about.

Her husband, according to William Matheson's genealogies in *The Blind Harper,* was Donald Morison, tacksman at Cross, who served as an ensign, on the Loyalist side, in the American War of Independence. He spent a good deal of the campaign locked up in Halifax gaol!

Matheson identifies him as the "half-pay ensign" who crossed the Minch in 1786 with John Knox, when Knox was touring the Highlands, gathering material for his report to the British Society for Extending the Fisheries. They set out from Stornoway on "a fine clear morning", making for Loch Ewe. By nightfall they were still off Loch Ewe, battling with a gale, and unable to make the harbour. They decided to run for Gairloch while Knox cowered in his cabin — "if it deserved that name" — furnished with a farthing candle which "afforded a glimmering light". Knox pled to be put ashore in the longboat, but was told they could "neither launch the boat, row on shore, or land with any prospect of safety."

Eventually they decided to run for Stornoway. At that point Knox fell into a deep and weary sleep. When he wakened in the morning, he asked Morison if they were near Stornoway. "Near Stornoway?" replied Morison. "We're still forty miles from it!" They had spent the night tacking back and fore off Gairloch, unable to get in to the anchorage, afraid to venture back into the open Minch. When the wind moderated, they made for Loch Ewe but were carried beyond the entrance almost to Loch Broom. They eventually made their way back to Loch Ewe, and landed at nightfall after something like 36 hours on the crossing.

Knox who was clearly scared out of his wits, pays tribute to the Lewis crew who "acquitted themselves with the perseverance, sobriety and ability for which their countrymen are so deservedly applauded." Morison, he adds, "like all the islanders, had some knowledge of sea affairs" and gave considerable assistance. "He amused himself, and us, through the day with mimickry and songs; but, when he saw the danger, he became serious, and flew to the work with great intrepidity." There was a point on the voyage when even Morison "became thoughtful". He overheard one of the crew say something to another in Gaelic, and realised there was a risk that the ship's timbers would not stand the strain.

If Lilias's husband was an old soldier with "some knowledge of sea affairs", her son was a Capt in the Royal Navy; her brother was a Lieut in the Navy, and her nephew, Kenneth Morison, was captain of an Atlantic liner, lost in mysterious circumstances which I will come back to in a later chapter, or a later book.

According to family tradition, Lieut John was a friend of Nelson. A casual dip into the Naval Records suggests that he took part in the battle of Copenhagen. Not long ago I had the pleasure of visiting his great-granddaughter, Mrs Biscoe, in her home in Inverness. A charming, hospitable lady, who had an interesting life herself, having travelled widely with her naval husband, and having been for some time a close companion of Gladys Aylward who wrote the story of the *Inn of the Sixth Happiness*. She still has in her possession, or in the safe hands of her bank, the walking stick given to her great grandfather by Nelson, and the linen sheets in which Prince Charlie had slept, on that troubled night at Arnish, when a "mob from Stornoway", anxious to see him away from their shores "made a dreadful noise about the house" for several hours.

Mrs Biscoe's link with Prince Charlie is through Lieut John Morison's wife, Christian. As William Matheson has explained it to me, Christian's father was Alexander MacIver, bailie of Stornoway. Her grandfather was also Alexander MacIver, bailie of Stornoway. The elder Alexander married Mary, daughter of Colin Mackenzie of Kildun, who was a grandson of the second Earl of Seaforth, and was taken prisoner at the battle of Sheriffmuir. He died in 1729 but his widow still lived at Arnish in 1746. She slaughtered one of her cows to feed the Prince's party, and provisioned his boat with meal, sugar and brandy before it sailed, under the very nose of a couple of frigates, lying off Kebbock Head. The Prince's ring, given in acknowledgement of that hospitality is also safely deposited in the bank.

Mr Matheson has reason to be familiar with the family history of the Mackenzies of Kildun. Before they came into possession of Arnish — which he prefers to spell, more correctly as Arinish — the tacksman there was his own great-grandfather's great-grandfather, John Matheson, known as Iain Arainis, who, he believes, was killed at the battle of Sheriffmuir.

Mrs Biscoe's family have cherished the link with the Prince over the generations. She told me that her father, who was called Charles Edward, was an ardent, if anachronistic, Jacobite. Every Hogmanay he drank a toast to "the King over the Water."

These associations with Nelson and Prince Charlie, and the American War of Independence, were all very much closer to Magaidh a' Chaiptein's grandmother than they are to us, and they must have figured prominently in her conversation.

While there is no direct link with the mutiny of the Bounty, Lilias was twenty-five years old when it took place. As a member of a well-educated, and much travelled, family she is bound to have known of it. Her brother would hardly have been in the navy by then — he was a good deal younger than Lilias. — and her son was still a baby, but both of them were in the navy in 1807, when James Morison lost his life, in circumstances which must have been discussed throughout the fleet, and which would have brought the whole history of his involvement in the mutiny back into general conversation.

Both brother and son returned to Lewis after their naval service, bringing with them the information they had. They would have known of any relationship with the mutineer, and it seems incredible they would have invented one, if it did not exist.

Besides, there is some circumstantial evidence that James Morison himself returned to Stornoway, for a time, after his trial and reprieve. If he did, Lilias Morison may well have met him personally, and heard the story from his own lips. In that case, her grand-daughter and confidante, Magaidh a' Chaiptein, would clearly have been "in a position to know".

3
Conversation in a Butcher's Shop

A casual conversation between two ladies in a butcher's shop in Stornoway brought me unexpected confirmation of my auntie Jessie's story that James Morison of the *Bounty* was a Lewisman. It brought more than confirmation, in fact. By providing, as it were, a cross-bearing on the mutineer, the new information told me precisely who he was.

My cousin, Ancrise Ross, and Rhoda Macleod from Knock, were discussing an article I had written about the *Bounty* for the *Stornoway Gazette*. Mrs Macleod mentioned that there was a tradition in her family that one of their relatives had been on the *Bounty*. I asked her for details, and was delighted to find that the Point tradition and the Stornoway tradition fitted each other like parts of a jig-saw puzzle.

Rhoda told me she had the information, as a young girl, from her father's first cousin, Christina Macmillan, of Swordale. Before sending the information to me, she took the precaution of checking with a neighbour — not related to the family — on Christina Macmillan's reliability as a bearer of tradition. The neighbour was horrified that she should doubt anything Christina had said.

"He said her father's house was the ceilidh house in the village, in his father's youth, and there were a couple of old sea captains in the village who used to pass down their tales."

From her own observation, Rhoda adds that Christina Macmillan "was a sharp tongued old lady who knew her facts, and would soon correct those who did not have them properly."

"She had a soft spot for me," she added, "because I was called after my father's only brother who was lost on the *Iolaire*. Many an hour I spent with her during school holidays in Swordale, enjoying her stories — but not the strong black tea!"

So here we have confirmation of the Lewis connection with the *Bounty*, preserved quite independently, in another part of the island, by relatives who had almost completely lost contact with my mother's family. The slender link that did remain between the families within living memory tends to buttress the tradition, as I will show.

Rhoda had assumed, as a child, that the mutineer's name was Mackenzie, because that was her father's name. It was only later in life, when she learned that one of her forebears, Murdo Mackenzie, the last tacksman in Aird, had married an Isabella Morison, she realised that the mutineer in her family tradition might well be James Morison.

9

More significant than the existence of the Point tradition is the correspondence between the details Rhoda can remember and known facts about my mother's family.

Christina Macmillan, she told me, "used to boast about the great seamen in the family. She used to refer to a captain who was lost on the English coast". The mutineer, she claimed, was an uncle of one of her progenitors, and there was a tradition that Kenneth Mackenzie, the son of Murdo Mackenzie and Isabella Morison, was taken to Knock by the tacksman there, "who was related to him", and given a piece of land. His job was to teach the farm hands to handle boats, and fish.

"He was in the sad position before he died," adds Rhoda, "to have lost two sons, John and Murdoch (my great-grandfather) in a drowning accident off Grimshader in 1851, and another son, Donald (father of the Cnoc Cuisbuig bard) off Portnaguran in 1859."

If we make the assumption that James Morison of the *Bounty* and Isabella Morison, who married Murdo Mackenzie, were brother and sister to my great-great grandfather, Angus Morison, everything falls neatly into place.

Angus Morison, according to William Matheson, is on record as having been one of the crew of a sloop, belonging to John MacIver, "bailie of Stornoway", when a drowning accident occurred on a voyage to Bergen in 1784. The reference occurs in a letter written by Rev John Downie, the minister of Stornoway, from his manse at Tong. He refers to Angus as "son of James Morison, Goathill", which anchors him firmly in our family tree.

Downie's letter establishes that the Morisons were a seafaring family around the date of the mutiny. It also establishes that James was a family name, which is specially pertinent because, as Matheson points out, "it is not a Morison or a Lewis name. Except for the Morisons it does not occur in Lewis in the 18th century save for a few 'aliens' (Munros etc) in Stornoway."

Angus's son, Roderick, my great-grandfather, was lost off Penzance, on the night of 28th August 1833, when the brig *Mary Ann,* of which he was mate, was wrecked on a voyage from Sydney Cape Breton. Presumably he was the "captain lost on the English coast," in Christina Macmillan's story.

On the assumption I have made, the mutineer would clearly have been an uncle of Christina Macmillan's forebears, as she said, and the tacksman who took Kenneth Mackenzie under his wing was almost certainly Lieut John Morison RN, brother of Lilias, and granduncle of Magaidh a' Chaiptein.

Although the Mackenzies in Point, descended from the mutineer's sister, and the Morisons in Stornoway, descended from his brother, had almost completely lost touch with each other until that conversation in the butcher's shop, Rhoda Macleod recalls from her youth that her grandaunt, known as Big Peggy used to visit relatives in Newton who were regarded as being rather "posh". While the epithet repels me, it could well have been applied, in the circumstances, to Mrs Pope, a captain's widow, and great-grandneice of the mutineer, who lived at No 1 Newton, or my grandfather, the mutineer's grand-nephew, who lived at No 29.

It is not out of perversity that I have pursued the identity of the mutineer in such great detail. It is of more than passing interest that the author of some of the most important source material, on the most famous of British naval mutinies, was a Gaelic-speaking Hebridean, and not a Londoner, as has been assumed for nearly two hundred years.

And it tells us a good deal about the social history of the Scottish islands that, when HMS *Bounty* sailed from Deptford on what was regarded as a very special mission by the Admiralty and, indeed, the Government as a whole, her crew of less than fifty included a Lewisman, an Orcadian and a Shetlander.

The Orcadian was one of the leaders of the mutiny. It was he who whispered to Fletcher Christian, at a crucial moment, "the people are ripe for anything." The Lewisman was, one might say, neutral in the mutiny. He made no effort to go with Bligh, but equally took no active part against him. The most damning evidence at his trial was his facetious shout, "If my friends enquire after me, tell them I am somewhere in the South Seas!" The Shetlander actually went with Bligh, and shared the miseries of the open boat voyage, but even he was logged by Bligh as a troublemaker. Clearly there was no bond of sympathy for a despotic captain, in the hierarchical tradition of an essentially English navy, on the part of Scottish islanders, used to a different style of personal relations and leadership.

In an earlier book I referred to the implications for our view of the state of education and literacy in the Hebrides, in the late 18th century, that Stornoway should have produced, in little over a decade, the greatest of the Canadian explorers, the first surveyor general of India, and the first person to write an extended account, in English, of life in Polynesia.

The place of the two Mackenzies in history is secure. Sir Alexander Mackenzie has been the subject of several biographies and his name is splattered over the map of Canada. Colin Mackenzie is also remembered despite the disappearance of the British Raj. While I was compiling the material for this book there was an Indian scholar at work in Lewis researching his background for a new biography. He is still a figure of some importance in the cultural life of the sub-continent.

Morison's notoriety as a mutineer has unfortunately obscured what should have been his fame as a reporter. The passages in his *Journal* which refer to the mutiny, and the events which led up to it, have been milked by scores, if not hundreds, of historians, novelists and film-makers, but the full text of his precise and racy account of life in Tahiti, before the impact of Western civilisation altered it, and to a large extent corrupted it, has been published only once — a hundred and thirty years after his death, when it had lost the impact of novelty and topicality.

It will now never command the attention, or achieve the reputation, it might have had, if it had been published when it was written, but we owe it to his memory to have it on the record that, when the London Missionary Society was founded, and the first English-speaking missionaries went to Polynesia, the vocabulary of "one hundred full-written folio pages," with the words alphabetically arranged and accented, which facilitated their work, had been compiled, in large part, by a bosun's mate from the Outer Hebrides, while he lay on board a prison ship, with the threat of execution hanging over his head.

4
The "King" was Poeno's Friend

Although there is no documentary evidence to support my identification of James Morison of the *Bounty,* such evidence as there is points in the right direction.

At his trial, Morison produced a letter from Capt Stirling, under whom he had served, as a midshipman, on HMS *Termagant.* Stirling wrote that Morison's conduct met with his entire approbation "for sobriety and attention to duty", adding specifically, "I ever found he paid due respect to his superiors, and that he was always obedient to commands."

Morison joined the *Termagant,* which appears to have been his first ship, when it was stationed at Leith. That should dispose of any lingering suggestion that he was a Londoner.

Charles Nordhoff and James Norman Hall, in their book *Mutiny,* speak of Morison, after his reprieve, as "bound for the north country." *Mutiny* is a novel, but the authors claim that all the incidents described are historically accurate, and that they had access to the private papers of Peter Heywood, who was condemned and reprieved along with Morison, worked with him in prison on the Tahitian vocabulary, and became the custodian of his *Journal.* Lady Belcher, Heywood's step-daughter, says that Morison was given three months' leave after his reprieve.

My guess is that these three months were spent in Lewis. No one who knew the story of the *Bounty,* only from the published record, would have dreamt of describing the mutineer as "king of a South Sea Island" — the phrase my uncle heard used in his youth — but I can think of no more likely description of the central figure in the lesser known parts of the *Journal,* if the adventures had passed into the oral tradition of acquaintances, listening to his own recital in the ceilidh house, or the pub. The Tahitian sections of the *Journal* — which were not accessible to anyone in Stornoway until more than half a century after the period my uncle was referring to, and a century and a half after the events described, — are the very stuff of legend.

Take almost any page from the *Journal* and transmute it from the written to the spoken word. Imagine the impact on his fellow islanders, listening to the man who, at that time, was the furthest travelled of them all: a man who had been in Australia in the year in which, according to the *Encyclopaedia Britannica,* Australian history was born.

His account of the Friendly Islands, for instance. "The natives flocked round the ship in great numbers to traffic for hogs, fowls and coconuts...

Several chiefs and principal men were constantly on board, and frequently not less than a hundred canoes of different sizes about the ship.

"Both sexes dress their hair with lime or burnt shells which, though originally black, soon turns to red, purple or white...The women are handsome, but know how to set a price on their favours.

"The men are tattooed from the knee to the waist which something resembles a pair of breeches. The women are not tattooed, but have on their shoulders several circles indented with burning hot bamboos of different sizes, and many of both sexes want a part, if not the whole, of their little fingers, which we understood were cut off as a tribute to the memory of their deceased friends."

At this point he might well have held up his own right hand, or the eyes of his listeners might have gone involuntarily to it, because he, too, for some unexplained reason, had lost the use of the upper joint of his fore finger. The injured finger, and a wound made by a musket ball in his arm, were among the points of identification listed by Bligh when Morison was still being hunted as a mutineer. He is described as being sallow complexioned, and of slender build, with long black hair. Under his left breast there was tattooed a star, and round his left leg a garter with the motto, "Honi soit que mal y pense".

An island audience, some of whom could still remember the 'Forty Five and the Butcher Cumberland, would have understood what he was getting at, when he criticised the insensitivity of Capt Bligh in making some of the local chiefs shell coconuts for his dinner, while he held them as hostages for the return of a grapnel that had been stolen.

They only smothered their resentment because they could not avenge the insult, he records, adding, perceptively, in a sentence which encapsulates the history of the British in Ireland, "If a weak-manned ship came in their way, they would remember this day's transactions and make them suffer for it."

The legend of the king of a South Sea Island would also have been fostered by Morison's nonchalent comment that, having made Poeno, Chief of the Matavai, his friend on his first visit to Tahiti, he went to live with him when he returned after the mutiny, being treated as one of the family, "but with more attention and respect".

On the island of Tubai, which they visited after the mutiny, Morison noticed part of a canoe which was clearly not of Tubai origin. He thought it looked like the canoes he had seen in Tahiti. His inquiries produced the information that the Chief of the district, Tummatoa, was a great-great-grandson of another Tummatoa, who had been driven to sea in a gale, from the island of Ryeatea, and didn't know how to find his way back. Later, in Tahiti, he was told by "the present Queen Dowager,"as he termed the Chief's mother, that her great-great-grandfather, called Tummatoa, had been King of Ryeatea, and was "blown away in a fishing boat and never heard of again."

Tummatoa's young son had accompanied the *Bounty* from Tubai to

Tahiti, and so, five generations after the separation, the family was reunited, thanks to the intervention of a bosun's mate from the Outer Hebrides. How a Lewis audience, still immersed in the traditions of the clans, would have loved that tale!

Morison took part in many of the local ceremonies under the guidance of his friend Poeno. Owen Rutter, who edited the only edition of the *Journal* ever published, comments that Morison was much more tolerant of the native customs and beliefs than Capt Cook.

For instance, when Morison and some of his companions were taken to pay their respect to the young King, they were told that he was still sacred, and could not be approached unless they stripped the clothing from their heads and shoulders.

Morison explained that "it was not customary to remove any part of our dress, except our hats, and, if we were under arms, it was not our country manner to remove our hat, even to the King." But, so that they would not seem deficient in respect to the Tahitians, it was suggested that they should each put on a piece of Tahitian cloth, over their normal garments, and remove that, before entering the ground the natives regarded as sacred.

Almost the last sentence in his Journal is criticism of a sailor, put ashore from a passing ship, for lack of courtesy to the natives. The sailor's offence was that he had carried food on his head, which was taboo in Tahiti. The Tahitians thought him "worse than a cannibal" but were prepared to excuse him "because he knew no better". It was true that he knew no better, says Morison, but it was also true that he tried to be "contrary to them in everything, which made him disagreeable to them all."

How well we know that type of incomer in the Highlands and Islands!

While he accepted the local customs, even to the extent of being present at ceremonies involving the human sacrifice of malefactors, Morison also tried to get the natives to understand that there were other, and higher, forms of religion.

"We kept the holidays in the best manner that we could," he writes, "killing a hog for Christmas dinner, and reading prayers, which we never omitted on Sundays."

"We informed the natives of our reasons for observing these holidays, and especially Christmas Day. They readily believed all that we could inform them of, never doubting that the Son of God was born of a woman, and they always behaved with much decency when present at our worship."

Some of them, he adds, "were desirous to have it explained to them. And some of them wished to learn our prayers which they all allowed to be better than their own."

"Those who were constantly about us knew when our Sunday came, and were always prepared accordingly. Seeing that we rested on that day, they did so likewise and never made any diversions on it.

"One of them was always ready to hoist the ensign on Sunday morning. And, if a stranger happened to pass, and enquired the meaning, they were

15

told it was 'Mahana Atooa' (God's Day), and though they were intent on their journey, would stop to see our manner of keeping it, and would proceed next day, well pleased with their information."

Morison was of opinion that the inhabitants of Tahiti were "without doubt the happiest on the face of the globe", but he had no wish to remain there permanently, and showed his determination to return to Britain in a very practical way.

5
Fire upon the Rascals!

Although Morison was only bosun's mate on the *Bounty* he was the natural leader in age, experience, education and general competence, among those of the crew who returned to Tahiti.

Most of the officers had gone off in the ship's launch with Bligh, to unleash the vengeance of the navy. Fletcher Christian, the senior officer among the mutineers, had gone to Pitcairn Island, taking the gunner's mate and one of the midshipmen with him. The party left on Tahiti consisted of nine ABs, the cooper, the armourer, the carpenter's mate, the master at arms, two midshipmen and Morison. One of the midshipmen was only 15 years old. The other was rated an AB on the ship's list although he messed with the midshipmen. The master at arms was roughly the same age as Morison — knocking on thirty — but he was an inveterate trouble-maker.

As I have already pointed out, Morison had been a midshipman himself, when he first joined the navy, but promotion to commissioned rank depended on influence, and it was not unusual for a midshipman to abandon the hope of ever becoming a lieut, and accept another post, as Morison had done, when he left HMS *Termagant* for HMS *Hind* "on promotion" as a gunner.

The report on his examination as a gunner, which survives, shows that he was a more than competent mathematician, and his activities on Tahiti suggest that he was a real all-rounder.

Not long after his return to the island, he began to think "it might be possible to build a small vessel" to reach Batavia and thence back to Britain.

He confided his plan to the carpenter's mate, and one of the ABs, but kept it secret from the others, saying the vessel he was building was "only for the purpose of pleasuring about the island." His precaution was necessary because several of them had acquired Tahitian wives, and had no wish to leave.

Looking ahead, Morison bought a quadrant, in exchange for a gallon of wine, from one of the crew who had somehow acquired the possessions of a midshipman who had gone with Bligh in the launch. The seaman also had some navigational books, although he could neither read nor write. He was using the pages for cartridge paper! When Morison began to bargain for the books, the seaman became suspicious and refused to sell.

"As I had a Seaman's *Daily Assistant* I took no further notice," writes

Morison, "and affected to be easy about them though I was sorry I could not get them".

The building of the boat was a Herculean task with the limited tools in their possession. They had to begin by felling trees in the forest, rafting them down to the coast, and sawing them up for keel, and ribs, and planks.

The work aroused great interest on the island. "Among our visitors came a blind man." writes Morison. "He examined the work by feeling every part, and asking the use and intention." He "seemed amazed at the construction of the vessel, of which he seemed to have a good idea, and said to his countrymen, 'our canoes are foolish things compared to this one'".

Morison's schooner had a 30 foot keel and was 35 feet over-all. The breadth at the midship frame was 9 feet 6 inches. Masts and sails were the most difficult items to provide. He and his companions made a "tolerably good" half-minute glass out of a phial, which they cut with a flint, and then made an azimuth compass with a small gourd as box.

They called the schooner, aptly, the *Resolution*.

In spite of the difficulties, their workmanship was good. Owen Rutter, in his introduction to the Golden Cockerel edition of Morison's *Journal*, says the *Resolution* had a fine turn of speed, and made one of the quickest passages ever known from China to the Sandwich Islands. Later it was used for surveying on the coast of China, and saved the lives of the crew of HMS *Providence* when it was wrecked off Formosa. But all that was of little consolation to Morison and the men who helped him build her.

Almost as soon as the *Resolution* was launched, HMS *Pandora* arrived at Tahiti in search of the mutineers. Morison, and those with him, immediately gave themselves up. Despite this, their hands were tied, and their legs were put in irons. Two seamen and a midshipman were posted over them with pistols and bayonets.

The Capt of the *Pandora*, Edward Edwards, had a reputation for harshness. In his very first command his brutality provoked a mutiny for which twenty men went on trial. Six were convicted and hanged, two were given up to five hundred lashes. The navy didn't believe in mollycoddling its men and life in the prison they called "Pandora's Box" was pretty grim.

"The first lieut, in trying the handcuffs," writes Morison, "took the method of setting his foot against our breasts and hauling the handcuffs over our hands with all his might, some of which took the skin off with them."

"All that could be hauled off by this means were reduced and fitted so close that there was no possibility of turning the hand in them, and when our wrists began to swell he told us that 'they were not intended to fit like gloves'"

When the *Pandora* struck a reef and was badly holed, Capt. Edwards gave pistols to the master at arms and a corporal, and told them to shoot the prisoners if they made any move to break their irons or escape. When they realised that the officers were abandoning the ship, some of the prisoners "began to stir" The master at arms heard the clank of their chains, and gave the order "Fire upon the rascals." Morison, who was near the hatch, shouted, "For God's sake don't fire. There is none here moving."

While the prisoners lay, in prison and in chains, on the sinking ship, they were able to see that the boats were being launched, and booms were being cut loose to make a raft. Then one of the topmasts fell into the waist of the ship, killing a man who was heaving the guns overboard to lighten her.

"Everything," writes Morison, "seemed to be in great confusion."

The ship was underwater as far as the main mast, and the sea was flowing into "Pandora's Box" before the bosun's mate answered the prisoners' cries and opened a scuttle.

"It was full as much as I could do to clear myself of the driver boom before the ship sunk," writes Morison.

He threw his trousers off, bound up his loins with a sash "in the Tahiti manner", grabbed a small plank, and set off to try to reach one of the boats. He was an hour and a half in the water before he was picked up. Then he learned that four of the prisoners had been drowned, and thirty-one of the crew. But all the officers were safe!

The *Pandora* was attempting to find a way through the Great Barrier Reef when she foundered. The survivors were faced with an open boat voyage of 1400 miles, along the north coast of Australia, to the nearest point where they could expect to pick up a vessel for Europe — the Dutch colony of Timor.

They landed on a key, or small spit of sand, for a few days after the shipwreck, to reorganise, before attempting the passage to Timor. A tent was pitched for the officers, and another for the men, but the prisoners were refused even a bit of sail to shelter them.

"The sun took such an effect on us, who had been cooped up for these five months, that we had our skins flayed off from head to foot, though we kept ourselves covered in sand during the heat of the day," writes Morison.

He added to his own discomfort by falling foul of Capt. Edwards, to whose launch he was assigned for the voyage to Timor.

"As I was lying on the oars talking to MacIntosh," he writes, "Capt Edwards ordered me aft, and, without assigning any cause, ordered me to be pinioned with cord and lashed down in the boat's bottom. Ellison who was then asleep in the boat's bottom was ordered the same punishment."

"I attempted to reason, and enquired what I had now done to be thus cruelly treated, urging the distressed situation of the whole, but received for answer, 'Silence, you murdering villain! Are you not a prisoner? You piratical dog, what better treatment do you expect?' I then told him it was a disgrace to the Captain of a British Man-of-War to treat a prisoner in such an inhuman manner. Upon which he started up in a violent rage, and, snatching a pistol which lay in the stern sheets, threatened to shoot me. I still attempted to speak when he swore, 'By God, if you speak another word, I'll heave the log with you.'"

Morison says he was tied down so that he could not move, and he remained in that "miserable situation" for the rest of the voyage.

When finally they got to Timor, the prisoners were put in the stocks in the Governor's castle. They were not even freed to relieve themselves. When they fell ill, the Dutch doctor refused to enter their prison until slaves were sent in to clean it out.

When they got to Spithead and were imprisoned on HMS *Hector*, conditions improved. Morison says "We were treated in a manner that renders the humanity of her captain and officers much honour."

Morison's account of Capt Edwards' brutality is confirmed by Sir John Barrow, who wrote the first full account of the mutiny. Barrow was a civil servant at the Admiralty, and founder of the Royal Geographic Society. He was writing about events of which he had contemporary knowledge, and he was not likely to be biassed in the mutineers' favour.

It was no doubt considerations like that which induced the Court Martial to recommend Morison "to His Majesty's Royal Mercy", when they found him technically guilty of mutiny, and imposed the only sentence they could — "death by hanging."

After his reprieve, and, as I believe, a sojourn in his native Lewis, where his tale would have aroused great interest, Morison returned to the navy.

His last ship was HMS *Blenheim*. Admiral Sir Thomas Troubridge, under whom Morison had previously served, specifically asked to have him as gunner on his flagship. It was a great tribute to the Lewisman's competence, but the consequences were unfortunate.

When Troubridge was transferred from India to the Cape, in 1807, he was advised that the *Blenheim* was no longer seaworthy. The stubborn old seadog said he would go to the Cape in his flagship, or not at all. The *Blenheim* sailed from Calcutta, and sunk off Madagascar with the loss of all on board.

As Owen Rutter wryly remarks, Morison "having nearly suffered hanging through the rancour of one commander, and drowning through the callousness of a second, finally met his end through the sentimental recklessness of a third."

20

6
Before Kon-Tiki

When Morison's Journal was published, for the first and only time, 119 years after he was drowned, I borrowed a copy from Birmingham City Library, through the good offices of Dan Macgregor, the librarian in Stornoway, and one of my closest friends. There didn't seem to be a copy available in any of the Scottish Libraries in the Carnegie scheme.

At that time my interest was a little detached because I was not convinced of the truth of my aunt Jessie's story. When I did realise that Morison was indeed a Lewisman, I tried to acquire a copy of the *Journal* for myself. It was a long hunt!

Eventually I located a copy in a second-hand bookshop in London, but the price was beyond anything I could afford to pay for a book. Only 350 copies had been published, and it is now a collectors' item with a price on its head.

Then I had a happy thought. When I was a student I had picked up a first edition of *Mackenzie's Voyages,* the book by another Lewisman which was smuggled out of London, as soon as it was printed, and translated into French, on Napoleon's orders, because he thought it might help with his plan to invade Canada along the Mississippi valley. Mackenzie's book, beautifully bound in leather, cost me £15, which doesn't seem much today, but which represented three weeks' salary at the rate of pay I had when I first became editor of the *Gazette.* I can still remember the sense of reckless extravagance with which I made the purchase.

Now I offered the bookshop in London to swop one Lewisman for another. I hoped that Mackenzie had appreciated in value over the years. The bookshop accepted the deal, and I got my copy of Morison's *Journal.* Parting with Mackenzie was like having my teeth out without an anaesthetic, but the loss was not absolute. There have been later editions of *Mackenzie's Voyages.* I lost the thrill of the leather binding, and the pride of possessing a first edition, but I did not lose the information the book contained.

On a second reading of the *Journal,* when I could take my time to it without worrying about library deadlines, my admiration for Morison was greatly increased. Morison the reporter rather than Morison the seaman!

Sir John Barrow describes Morison as "a person from talent and education, far above his station on the *Bounty".* Owen Rutter says he was "a born writer" and "a shrewd observer of human nature" with "a literary ability uncommon in seamen of his time." Rutter adds that Morison "had an insatiable curiosity and the knack of recording exact information with a wealth of picturesque detail".

He was interested in everything. The appearance and dress of the natives. Their customs. Their religious observances. The design of their canoes, and the variations in design between the different islands. Even when he was bound hand and foot, on a Dutch vessel, on the voyage from Batavia to the Cape, his investigative mind was noting the differences between the Dutch and British procedure in victualling ships, and calculating how much the canny Dutch were making, out of the prisoners, by stretching a fortnight's rations over 16 days.

He also indulged in some philosophical speculations about the origins of the Polynesians, anticipating, by a century and a half, ideas that have enjoyed a vogue in our own day.

Shortly after the publication of Thor Heyerdahl's account of the Kon-Tiki expedition I saw his raft in Oslo, in the museum where it is now preserved. I remember standing, with a small block of Balsa wood in one hand and a block of greenheart in the other, astonished that two apparently identical bits of wood could weigh so differently. Heyerdahl's voyage from Peru to Tahiti, with a parrot and five companions, on a primitive balsa-wood raft, such as the Indians used, was inspired by his theory that Polynesia was peopled from South America. The success of the voyage, he says, does not prove that his theory is correct, but it does prove that it is possible.

Describing how the theory gradually took hold of him as he studied the matter, he writes, "Both my suspicions and my attention were turned more and more away from the Old World, where so many had searched and none had found, and over to the known and unknown Indian civilisations of America, which no one hitherto had taken into consideration."

No one hitherto? There it is, in two sentences, in Morison's *Journal:* "The inhabitants of those islands drive about in their canoes to an amazing distance, and I am therefore led to think that the whole of the islands in these seas might have been peopled from South America. Notwithstanding the difference of their language, manners and customs (all of which are liable to change in length of time) yet the present languages of all the islands in these seas differ no more than English does in different counties."

In the immediately preceding paragraph Morison has another very acute observation, which might almost be said to encapsulate the essential seed in Arnold Toynbee's philosophy of history, based on the belief that "the cause of the genesis of civilisations must be sought in a pattern of interaction", which he called "challenge and response".

Puzzling over the problem that, although he believed the South Sea Islanders all came from the same stock, they differed widely in manner, custom, appearance, and particularly in the presence or absence of a desire to improve, by using the white man's technology, Morison writes, "Perhaps this may be occasioned by the different degrees of fertility of the islands". Then comes the crucial passage: "The inhabitants of those isles where every necessary is supplied by nature have no occasion to cultivate the earth, and are less robust and vigorous than those who have exercise and labour in producing their food."

I have suggested elsewhere that the conjunction of Morison and the two Mackenzie explorers in the history of Lewis implies that there was a teacher of more than usual ability in Stornoway, in the middle years of the 18th century. It may be necessary to go even further than that.

Many years ago old Murdo Maclean, the shipping agent, and father of my cousin Stephen, asserted, to my surprise, that a lad in his native Uig in 1800 would have been better educated than a lad in Uig in 1900. His thesis — a provocative one — was that the Disruption set education back for fifty years in the islands, because children no longer went to the parish schools, maintained by the Established church, and it was some considerable time before their place was filled by other schools of comparable quality.

He told me that Angus Macritchie, grandfather of one of my contemporaries, Dr Angus Macleod, had told him he could remember boys sneaking off to school, in his youth, against their parents' wishes. On at least one occasion he saw a boy being hoisted on to the back of an older brother, while his father thrashed him, for daring to go to the parish school.

In the course of the same conversation, Murdo told me that there was an old building, down by the shore in Brenish, in his own day, which was pointed out as the school in which Lord Macaulay's great-grandfather had been educated. I often regret that I was never in Brenish with Murdo to have the old school pointed out to me.

Even if Murdo's comments on Uig are true they are not necessarily relevant to conditions in Stornoway, but there does seem to have been a history, perhaps a somewhat intermittent history, of good education in the town. Agnes Mure Mackenzie — a patriotic Lewiswoman — comments, in one of her histories, that Greek was taught in Stornoway before it was taught in the High School of Edinburgh.

We tend to think of the Scottish Enlightenment of the 18th century as a scintillation of stars, like David Hume and Adam Smith, but it is possible that a good deal more than is generally allowed percolated down to the grass roots. Or even that the great names of the period represent the cream on a well-filled jug of educational milk.

Be that as it may, there is another element in the story of the bosun's mate. He belonged to a family with a very long tradition of higher education. William Matheson's genealogical tree includes quite a surprising number of university graduates, from a very early date, and not all of them clergymen.

There also runs through the family a facility with words, sometimes in Gaelic, sometimes in English, sometimes in both, generally in prose but also frequently in verse. Not poetry, properly so-called, but light satirical verse.

Matheson devotes a long and fascinating appendix to the snatches of verse attributed, in the Lewis tradition, to John Morison of Bragar, ranging from mildly unflattering comments on his wife and servants, and the town of Stornoway, to a savage lampoon on a priest who forgot his office so far as to get his host's daughter with child.

So far as I know, James Morison of the *Bounty* did not write poetry, but his facility with words, and his innate urge to observe and report, do nothing to disprove my claim that he was descended from John Morison of Bragar, and An Clarsair Dall, and was a not-too-distant cousin of his great contemporary, Zachary Macaulay, the historian's father.

7
The Golden Ring of Palmyra

James Morison was the first Lewisman to sail in the South Pacific of whom I have any record, but, since his day, many Lewis seamen have become more familiar with these distant waters than with their own crofts. Notable among them Bosun Kenneth Stewart from Tong, who was the sculptor's model for the national war memorial of the Merchant Navy, erected on Tower Hill in London. The sculptor's choice was, no doubt, determined by Stewart's magnificent physique, but it was also a fitting tribute to the remarkable contribution Lewis seamen made to the work of the Merchant Navy in the Hitler War.

Midway between James Morison and Kenneth Stewart, another Lewisman, Donald Macdonald, son of a Bernera man who had been headmaster in Bayble, made an open boat voyage from Palmyra to Samoa, which earned him the coveted bronze medal of Lloyds for his "extraordinary exertions to rescue the crew and passengers" of the *Henry James* which was shipwrecked on an uncharted reef with a cargo of coal, a crew of 19 and 11 passengers, including women and children.

After the loss of the *Henry James,* on which he had been mate, Macdonald came home to Lewis and lived for a year with an aunt. During that time he said nothing about his own part in the rescue. It only became known when he was summoned to Glasgow to receive his medal. Nearly forty years later, however, in his retirement, in New Zealand, he sat down to write an account of the incident for a relative in Sandwick who had pressed him for it. I can still remember my excitement, as a schoolboy in my late teens, when my father brought home, one lunchtime, the letter which he had borrowed, with its graphic, but modest, account of one of the great voyages in the history of the Merchant Navy.

"At midnight the ship ran on a reef which was not on our charts. My watch was below at the time, but it only took seconds to get on deck... I swung the foreyards round but she did not move. She was hard and fast. She commenced to labour as there was a heavy swell pounding her... It was impossible to launch the forward lifeboats, so the two after boats were launched, and we stood by her until daylight with hopes to board her. But it was hopeless. The sea was heavy all round. There was nothing left for us except to make for Palmyra Island, which we had passed the day before, and which was now fifty miles distant."

"The Captain was in charge of the cutter and I was in the gig. The sea was heavy for the boats. I had ten seamen with me. The Captain had twenty in his boat, the women and children as well, and, as I was carrying all sail, my boat was much faster, sailing two miles for his one. In the afternoon I sighted the island, exchanged signals, and then pressed the boat for the land. The wind was increasing, but I got close in and stopped for the other boat to come up. To my surprise the Captain gave orders to stop out all night, as it was not prudent to approach the island. I disobeyed and made sail, and on making two tacks I found a landing, so the other boat followed, and we got ashore as night set in… The first thing we did was to offer thanks for our deliverance."

And deliverance it was! A tropical storm blew up during the night. If they had remained in the boats they would have perished within sight of land. Not that there was much comfort for them on Palmyra. There were plenty of birds but they could find no water. The Captain asked Macdonald to go to Samoa for help, a distance of 1630 miles.

"I asked him to show me the course. He had the chart. The course was S.S.W. straight for the island. I saw at once the danger of it, and asked him 'If I run down the latitude and find no land there, on which hand will I look for the island?' He burst out crying, and I refused to have anything to do with it."

The next day they all went out looking for fresh water. In the evening Donald came back to the camp "tired, hungry and miserable". His brother John, who was the ship's carpenter, was with him.

"As I sat down, one of the girls was eating a raw bird. It 'came against her' and, as she was retching badly, she threw herself in my lap and fell asleep. My brother stroked the child's feet with his hands, and, remarking to me, 'She is not long for this world!', burst out crying. As she awoke she was crying, telling how hungry she was. The sight before me was thrilling. I spoke to her, and told her not to cry, as it was no use. I took my gold ring from my finger, and put it on her finger, saying to her, 'Don't cry. I am going away with the boat, and I will get food for you to eat.' She ran and told her mother of what I had said to her."

Having made up his mind, Donald called the bosun and told him to secure the mast in the bigger boat, in the morning, with stays for hard driving, and to send all hands out to gather coconuts, as that was the only food they had.

As they were getting the boat ready, the Captain came over and began to give orders as to how many men he should take. Donald asked if the Captain was going with them. When he said 'No', Donald said, "In that case, leave me alone!"

"Friday night was to be my last night on this earth and I warned everyone to keep clear of me, as I wanted to rest. I lay down under the boat that was to be my grave, but I found that sleep had deserted me, so I got up and crossed the bottleneck of the island as far as the sea would allow me. I was in terrible distress, and like good old Job, I cursed my days — in Gaelic: 'C'ar son a ghabh na Guinean romham? Agus c'ar son na ciochan, gu'n deothailinn?'

"I had no one to advise me or help me, so I went on my knees pouring out my trouble...I passed the night in that position, asking God to guide me in my undertaking. As I got up, my brother met me. I told him of all my plans and the track I was to take. I warned him not to go in the boat. Then I went to the Captain."

When he called for volunteers to go with him in the boat, three Irish sailors and an American stepped forward. One of the Irishmen was very young, so Donald asked a German sailor to take his place, which he did. He told them to be ready at noon. Took an altitude of the sun, and made for the boat. The little girl's mother stood in his path, "a block of silence".

"I could not speak. I put my hand on her shoulder and kissed her on the cheek, but she followed me to the boat. As I took my place in the boat, I waved my hand to let go the painter, and swung the boat's head towards the open sea, amidst the heart-rending prayers and pitiful petitions of the helpless group that was kneeling on the rough coral island — a sad parting on the banks of Palmyra."

When they got clear of the island, and set the sail, the sea was very confused. As the island was dipping, and he took his departure course, a heavy squall struck them, carrying the rudder away. The boat broached and filled.

The weather continued very rough for several days, but then they got "a slashing breeze." In a single day they covered 132 miles and crossed the Equator. In 4 degrees south they ran into a frightful thunderstorm, and found, to their horror, that the milk in the coconuts had turned thick and green — pure poison. They were eight hundred miles from the nearest land with nothing to eat or drink, except a few old dry coconuts which they nibbled once a day. Donald had to abandon the favourable course he had been following, and pick a straight course for Samoa. The hard driving was beginning to tell on the boat, and they had to throw some of the ballast overboard.

They had only one pair of boots between them. They cut them up and chewed them to make the saliva flow. When they had eaten the boots, they ripped the leather cover off the telescope and chewed that. Their tongues were swelling and cracking. Their lips were throbbing in the heat. Their bodies mere shells. Two of the sailors were now done out — the German and the American. One morning, when Macdonald went to relieve the helmsman, he found him sucking his own blood. He did not blame the man. He thought him a noble fellow. He could so easily have cut a piece of flesh from one of the men lying unconscious at his feet.

As daylight appeared on the 18th day, Macdonald noticed what looked like a black cloud right ahead on the horizon.

"As the sun got up, I made sure that it was land — a land of promise if ever there was any. In fact, I was looking for it, but did not mention it to anyone. The bosun then came aft and, in a whisper, said 'There's an island on our beam'. I collected all the coolness I could muster, and said, 'That island is Manua'. Then I pointed to him Samoa, straight ahead, and told him to take the helm, so that I could get the bearings. I found it to be 54 miles off.

"As I took the helm again, these poor fellows gathered round me, doing all the honour now left to them. But none of them could speak. The tears of thankfulness ran down their faces."

The breeze was light all day, and at midnight it fell dead calm. Then there was a sudden storm with thunder and lighting. They had to stand off to the southward till daylight. In the morning they sighted a schooner belonging to one of the Samoan chiefs. He was amazed when they told him they had come from Palmyra, but he took them into harbour and had them carried to the British consul.

Two or three days later, Macdonald set sail for Palmyra again with the three fittest of his companions, on a schooner put at their disposal by the British consul. They had a terrible voyage against adverse winds. It took them 28 days to reach Palmyra. There was no one there! Then they found a note to say that the survivors had been taken off by the mail steamer *Mariposa.* An American lieutenant, who was in Samoa on the day Macdonald landed, and who heard his story, alerted the *Mariposa,* and the Captain made a detour of 1500 miles to pick them up.

Eight years later, when he was mate on the *Auldgirth* of Glasgow, lying at the quay in Portland, Oregon, Macdonald saw two young women approach the gangway. One of them asked whether he had been mate on the *Henry James.*

"Well, ladies, I saw the last of that ship," he said.

She then drew off her glove, took a ring from her finger, and handed it to him. It was his own!

"Putting my hands on her shoulders I said, 'Then you are Laura Mary Hastings.'

Between sobs she answered, 'I am, sir, and this is my sister, Ada.'"

8
Toy and Tallahassee

The rescue of the crew and passengers of the *Henry James* might seem adventure enough for one lifetime, but it was a small part of Donald Macdonald's story. Some years ago I was sent a copy of *Sea Breezes* in which an old shipmate of his recalled how he had saved the *Dallam Tower* when it was dismasted. Donald Macdonald, the writer added, was shipwrecked nine times, and had twice been the sole survivor.

He was mate of the barque *Killochan,* lying off the mouth of the Thames, under easy sail, waiting for the tide, when she was run down and cut almost in two, by a German steamer. Macdonald was asleep when the collision occurred. The impact put out his lamp, and he could not find the door. Eventually he got out, but the ship sank under him as he was climbing the poop ladder. He was caught in the mizzen rigging, and dragged down, his arm badly torn. When he came to the surface he was close to the steamer. Fortunately she was in ballast, high out of the water, and he was able to hang on to the stationary propeller until his shouts were heard.

He had such a run of bad luck, according to the writer in *Sea Breezes,* he would never take a command, although he had his extra master's ticket. "Like most unlucky people he lived to die ashore."

His later years were spent in New Zealand where he lived in a little timber house built by his brother, John, the ship's carpenter, who had been with him on several voyages. Their sister and her daughter lived nearby. Recently I had letters from two of his New Zealand neighbours who remembered him well, although he died more than half a century ago.

"He was born in Stornoway", writes Cecil Burgess. "His father was a schoolteacher and his mother a Harris woman, very clever with linen and tweed handicrafts. Both were dead by the time Donald was 17, and he had to support his two sisters and six brothers by working on the herring boats which, he said, meant a very Spartan existence. I still recall many visits as a lad to the old cottage where Donald told many tales of his life at sea. He was very kind to children, and a visit to him always ended with a steaming cup of tea with biscuits and honey."

A younger neighbour, Mrs Clarice Newlands, writes that Donald taught her "all the knots" when she was a child, so that she could pass her Girl Guide tests. He used to cook fish for the family when her mother was ill.

So far as my informants are aware, there are no relatives of the family in New Zealand now, but his Lloyds medal is preserved in Waitaki Boys High School, in Omaru, where he spent his retirement.

Donald Macdonald's cousin, Murdo Stewart Macdonald from Bernera, was even better known as a captain in the days of sail, although his career was not quite so fraught with disasters. He earned the soubriquet "Last of the Sea Barons". In his early twenties, MacCunn of Greenock offered him command of the *Sir Lancelot* which with the *Cutty Sark* and the *Thermopylae* must rank as the greatest of the China Clippers. On his first outward voyage he sailed from Greenock to Java in 65 days, a record that has never been beaten.

On another occasion, he left Calcutta for Bombay in company with another clipper bound for the same port. *Sir Lancelot* found good winds which the other vessel missed, and they met up again, off the coast of Ceylon, when Macdonald was on his way back to Calcutta and his friend was still on the outward voyage.

The vessels ranged alongside, with main yards aback, to exchange their news. Nothing was said about the trip until Macdonald gave the command, "Fill on the main yards, and square away!"

The other Captain was still within earshot. "Square away?" he shouted. "Whatever for? I thought you were bound for Bombay."

"Not now!" shouted Macdonald. "I have a cargo of salt for Calcutta."

When he retired from the sea Murdo Stewart Macdonald became Lloyds agent in Port Louis, Mauritius. I used to correspond with him occasionally, when I first took over the *Gazette* from my father, and I heard even more about his career from one of his friends, who had no connection with Lewis, but wrote nautical articles under the nom de plume *Cappy Ricks.* It was odd, but not untypical, that a small local newspaper in what the world regards as a backwater, in the Outer Hebrides, should have a nautical correspondent in Mauritius.

Not long ago, when I addressed a seminar of civil servants from overseas, studying local government at Birmingham University, I asked one of the party, who came from Mauritius, if he knew Murdo Stewart Macdonald, or Dr de Lingen, who had been my minister in Stornoway, and who, I knew, had spent some years in Mauritius. He told me he had heard of Macdonald but did not know him. De Lingen had been his father's best friend!

Unlike Donald Macdonald, who has left no relatives in New Zealand whom I can trace, Murdo Stewart MacDonald has many descendants in Mauritius. Nigel Fisher in his biography of Iain Macleod recalls that MacLeod visited Mauritius when he was Secretary for the Colonies. "There was no political motive for the visit, but there was a personal one," writes Fisher. "It so happened that his great-uncle had retired to Mauritius many years before, and Macleod had no less than sixty-three relations living on the island."

The great-uncle was Murdo Stewart Macdonald, Last of the Sea Barons. And so even a busy Cabinet Minister, engaged in the delicate task of unscrambling an empire with the minimum of fuss and rancour, got caught up in the Lewis web: the worldwide network of tenuous but durable links which hold the extended community together.

Both Iain Macleod's parents were from Lewis. He spent most of his boyhood holidays on the island and wrote many poems to express his love for it. After his death, his widow acknowledged the strength of the tie by taking a Lewis title when she became a baroness — Baroness Macleod of Borve. It is a difficult island to break away from.

While Donald Macdonald's medal is preserved in New Zealand, and Murdo Stewart Macdonald's descendants still thrive in Mauritius, the snuff box presented by the Stornoway Trades Society, to the man who taught navigation to most of the Lewis sea captains of the period is now in Tallahassee, in Florida.

I learned of the existence of the snuff box from John MacKay Shaw, the great-grand-nephew of John Mackay, in whose school, on the corner of Keith Street and James Street, grown men, with the salt of distant seas still caked on their faces, sat among the children as they studied for their mate's or master's certificates.

Mackay was known as "Toy" because of his diminutive size but he was a big man in the life of the town. W. C. Mackenzie, who had known him in his boyhood, describes him as "a little man with a solemn face, looking as if he had all the cares of the town on his shoulders. He might have been a Regency portrait stepped out of its frame, with his antiquated top-hat, his high pointed collar and his tail-coat of soberest black".

Annie Macaulay Jamieson in *The Old Lewis Guard* describes John Mackay, distributing food to visitors, after an open air communion service on the Green — later the playground of the Francis Street building of the Nicolson Institute. "His hands would be laid kindly on their shoulders, they would look up and see a face they could not forget: a face lighted by dark eyes full of purpose, but, at the same time, soft and appealing". "In his nautical class" she adds, "the same face was full of command and will", especially when he took his class down to Sandwick Beach to teach them to handle the sextant.

Mrs Jamieson's book is an odd compilation, but characteristic of Lewis. Her theme is intensely parochial — the stalwarts of the evangelical movement in Lewis in the nineteenth century, *"The Old Lewis Guard"* — but her book begins with a description of "the splendid nights" of Italy with "an almost tropical moon". Later she refers familiarly to "the garden of the Pacific", to Mexico "where the wings of birds flash and close and flash again like an explosion of burning colour", and to "Carmel's bold bluff", "where Lewis sailors have often been, near the borders of Palestine." In Jamaica and Cuba, she adds, all her writing was done "in small quiet ports and picturesque towns".

She appears to have been in San Francisco shortly after the great earthquake and fire of 1906, which devastated four square miles of the city. At least she refers to "a harbour of indescribable beauty", "but now no houses, no streets", a scene of desolation which, she says, reminded her of a powerful sermon preached in the Free Church, in Stornoway, by Peter Maclean from the text, "Repent, or else I will come quickly and I will remove thy candlestick out of its place".

It seems to have been the habit of Stornoway sea captains to take their wives with them on voyages in those days. Mrs Jamieson describes an occasion when she was entertained, in a foreign port, by "a Bayhead boy" — Capt Colin Maciver — and his wife, on board the *Arrow*, "an Anglo-American oil ship, a 5000 ton four masted barque."

Mrs Maciver features in my earlier book *Surprise Island*. She was the Mrs Hong Kong of my youth, whose efforts to rise from the pew in church with a "yo heave ho" so much amused my brother and myself.

Mrs Jamieson lists the "shipmasters of the old town" in her young days — Robertsons, Macivers, Mackenzies, Munroes, Morisons, Macleods, Macaulays, Smiths, Macdonalds and Macleans, all in the plural, with Murray, Forbes, and Pope, in the singular, to round them off.

The list calls to mind my auntie Bella's story, told me in her hundredth year, that there were eleven captains in her little bit of Newton when she was a girl, but a neighbour's son always insisted there were twelve. There were carters as well as seamen in the street, and the twelfth Captain was a horse!

And that takes me back to my granny's old home on the seafront at Newton, where this all began with my auntie Jessie's story about the mutiny of the Bounty.

I have still to pick up her stories about Mac an t-Sronaich and the Claw.

9
A "Black" Santa Claus

When my old teacher, Alex Urquhart, asked the pupils in his Gaelic class to write an essay on Mac an t-Srònaich, just a few years after I had left the Nicolson, he got a great wealth of material. The outlaw was then a living legend in the island. More real than Napoleon or Wellington, who only existed in history books. More real even than Baldwin and Ramsay Macdonald, who existed only in the newspapers. He was a sort of inverted Father Christmas. On the analogy of black comedy, one might call him a black Santa Claus. An evil man, in whom we all implicitly believed, even if the stories about him were highly improbable.

One of the stories in Alex Urquhart's collection relates to the murder of a little boy. This is a favourite. Mac an t-Srònaich is reputed to have murdered many boys. In many places. But, in the end of the day, they all come down to the one archetypal child. The story always ends, "He said on the gallows that he regretted nothing he did but the murder of that poor child."

We even have the precise words he was supposed to have used — in four lines of Gaelic poetry. Rhyming was in the family, as I have said, but it seems a little excessive to compose a poem as you murder a child.

If Mac an t-Srònaich had been executed, and had made a speech from the scaffold, it might well have been reported, as the speeches of other notorious criminals were. The odd thing is that his dying words survive in the oral tradition of people who could not possibly have been present, but not in any written record, such as one might expect in regard to a murderer whose reputed toll far exceeds that of Manuel or the Yorkshire Ripper.

In the story of the murdered child we not only have the words supposed to have been spoken from the gallows, when there would have been by-standers, but the words spoken by the dying child, when there was no one present but the two of them, and Mac an t-Srònaich was pushing his victim into a deep dark pool, in the middle of the moor, with a stout oak stick. Who was the reporter on that occasion?

According to one version, the lad was murdered near Leurbost, at a spot where there is a cairn and not a blade of grass grows even to this day — just as the child predicted.

In another version of the same story, the lad, in his attempt to escape, swam not one loch but three, and the lochs are on the Barvas Moor — Gunnabhat, Eile-bhat and Loch an Fheòir.

Mac an t-Srònaich is supposed to have claimed his final victim when he

33

was actually standing before the judge waiting to be sentenced. He was accused of nineteen murders. "Why did you not make twenty of it?" asked the judge ironically. Mac an t-Srònaich asked for a drink of water. Then brained a by-stander with the iron vessel in which it was given to him saying to the judge as he struck the blow, "There's your twentieth!"

There is a particularly gruesome story about the murder of a bridegroom from Back. The man had gone to town for whisky for his wedding. He and his friend were straggling home, heavily laden, when Mac an t-Srònaich fell in with them. By a ruse he got them separated from each other. Killed the bridegroom. Then thrust the fragments of the piggy, in which he was carrying the whisky, into his flesh so that, when he was found, people would think he had fallen on the piggy and killed himself by accident.

There are just as many stories about the way Mac an t-Srònaich was captured as there are about the murders he committed. If he was captured as frequently as the legends say, he must have been a greater escapologist than Houdini.

One of the most circumstantial of the capture stories has clearly suffered a time shift of something like half a century. It begins with two brothers from Ness coming home across the moor from their training with the "Reserve" in Stornoway.

The older brother became tired and went to rest in a sheiling, while the younger continued home. In the sheiling the older brother was set upon by Mac an t-Srònaich who was sheltering there, and killed.

As soon as the younger brother got home he became anxious. Guessed what had happened. And set of for the sheiling, curiously armed with a stocking stuffed with paper and shells.

When he got to the sheiling, he threw the stocking on the floor. Mac an t-Srònaich thought, by the sound, the stocking was full of money, and bent to grab it. The Niseach produced a cudgel from his sleeve, which must have been remarkably capacious, and knocked Mac t-Srònaich on the head.

He hurried back to the village for reinforcements to seize the murderer, but, by the time they reached the sheiling, he was gone.

However, they were able to follow him across the moor by a trail of blood. It led to an old woman's house, but she denied having seen him. Just as they were about to leave, the younger brother saw a bloodstain on the top of the meal chest.

When the lid was lifted, there was Mac an t-Srònaich, cowering on top of the meal, with blood streaming from his ear.

On an other occasion he was captured, not by a brawny naval reservist from Ness, but a minister's maid from Uig. In the Uig story Mac an t-Srònaich was being entertained in the manse on the best of food and drink. Not an angel unawares, but a murderer.

When his appetite was satisfied, he took out his knife and lunged for the maid. She eluded him and fled from the house, with Mac an t-Srònaich in hot pursuit.

She was quick enough to get round the end of the barn without being seen. He thought she had gone into it, and stormed in after her. Smartly she slammed the door, bolted him in, and sent for the cops.

Oddly, there always seemed to be "officers" at hand to effect an arrest, although, in Mac an t-Srònaich's day, Lewis must have been very inadequately policed. As a child I believed quite firmly that he had been arrested, and hung on Gallows Hill, which I could see from my granny's house in Newton.

I also believed — as every child in Stornoway believed — that the cave at the mouth of the River Creed had been his hideout. The flat slab of rock inside the cave had been his bed. The huge rectangular block of stone just outside the door had been his table. I missed the irony of my childish belief, that the arch criminal had his lair at the very foot of Gallows Hill.

About the same time as I ceased to believe in Santa Claus, I lost my faith in Mac an t-Srònaich. With the sophisticated eyes of an eight-year-old I could see that the story of the cave was quite absurd.

Then, out of the blue, when I was a grown man, Auntie Jessie announced that Mac an t-Srònaich had really existed. Her granny, or grandaunt, used to leave food for him in the scullery window of her home, at the junction of Kenneth Street and Bayhead. And, when I asked Willie Matheson if he believed in Mac an t-Srònaich, he replied with devasting assurance, "He was a relative of yours."

While Lewis legend treats Mac an t-Srònaich as a nickname — the son of the man with the prominent nose — Matheson regards it as a patronymic.

Mac an t-Srònaich had a nose "like a shinty stick" avers one of Alex Urquhart's essayists, in a picturesque phrase. Alex Urquhart himself adds, "who he was or where he came from is known of him no more than of Melchizedek".

"Not so!" says Matheson, in effect. Mac an t-Srònaich was his real name, in Gaelic. He was a son of Alexander Stronach, innkeeper at Garve, whose wife Nancy (or Ann) was a daughter of John Morison, (Iain Mór mac a' Mhinisteir), a merchant and fish-curer in Stornoway, tacksman first of Little Bernera, and later of Druimchork, Gruinard.

So here we have the ogre of my youth clothed with flesh and blood. Given "a local habitation and a name". But what exactly he did to justify his fearsome reputation, and what became of him, are questions to which the answer seems to be both prosaic — and puzzling!

10
Mac an t-Srònaich was a "Fantom"

The one thing we know with some certainty about Mac an t-Srònaich is that he was not executed on Gallows Hill, as I had fondly believed. Local executions in Lewis had come to an end long before the period in which he flourished.

It seems equally unlikely that he was executed in Inverness, which is the venue of his death-bed speeches in many of the versions of the tale.

It is always difficult to prove a negative but a careful study of the *Inverness Courier* for the relevant period reveals no record of a mass murderer being hanged for crimes committed in Lewis. Nor is there any reference to a reign of terror in the island or a spate of unexplained murders or even assaults.

The *Inverness Courier* at the time covered events in the Western Isles fairly thoroughly, ranging from a lengthy account of the evictions in Uist to a racy description of the sea serpent which appeared in Broad Bay in 1830. That must have been pretty close to the time the two-legged monster we are investigating also made his appearance.

The *Courier* didn't take the sea serpent too seriously but it did say it couldn't have been a whale because it didn't "blow". Besides it had a mane like a horse. Only it was white and very much longer than a horse's. The sea serpent was from 60 to 80 feet long and was watched by fishermen for a fortnight.

The only murder from Lewis in the relevant years relates to a man described as a maniac who killed his neighbour by striking him on the head with a spade. His name was John Smith, and at his trial in Inverness, the local doctor — Dr Millar — confirmed that he was mad. He had known him for some years and he did not even have lucid interludes. The charge against him was dropped, but he was still committed to gaol. It was probably the only place the authorities had for a mentally disturbed person in those days.

Coincidentally, the next time I will have occasion to refer to Dr Millar is in connection with another murder, committed far from Lewis, on the high seas.

If there is no evidence that Mac an t-Srònaich was arrested, and hanged, for a murder committed in Lewis, is it possible that he was on the run for a murder committed elsewhere, before he sought refuge in the Lewis bogs?

Again the most one can say is that there is nothing in the *Courier* files which points in that direction.

Around the appropriate period there was a pedlar murdered in the snow near Grantown. It is the sort of crime which is attributed to Mac an t-Srònaich in local tradition. But the Grantown murderer spoke with a south-country accent.

Another more likely incident occurred near Invergordon. An elderly spinster living by herself, and believed to have money in the house, was brutally murdered and her house ransacked.

The murderer seems to have known her movements. He caught her half way between her own house and her neighbour's. The place was systematically searched. Trunks and boxes were wrenched open. Letters and papers were strewn on the floor. There was no clear indication that money was taken, but clothes, table linen and other household goods were missing.

The *Courier* comments that it was the first crime of that kind in Easter Ross for more than twenty years, and adds that "strong suspicions are entertained against some individuals."

The locus of the crime was not too far from Mac an t-Srònaich's father's inn, but, if he had been involved, would he have given himself away by fleeing to Lewis before there was a warrant out for his arrest? I found no evidence in the *Courier* of a hue and cry.

Sadly I have been driven to the conclusion that the innumerable murders attributed to my relative by my fellow islanders existed only in their imaginations. Alex Urquhart, I think, put his finger on the truth when he was preparing a paper for the Gaelic Society of Inverness, based, in part, on the Nicolson essays. In Stornoway Sheriff Court he unearthed a warrant, dated 1834 (which seems in the right time bracket), for the arrest of a man, said to be "lurking about the island of Lewis", putting the inhabitants of the island "in fear for their lives." Terrorising, it would appear, but not killing.

The one story among the many I have heard about Mac an t-Srònaich which has the ring of truth, corresponds with the Sheriff Court warrant both in substance and in time.

According to the tradition Mac an t-Srònaich waylaid an Arnol woman, on her way home from Stornoway, across the moor, no doubt laden with purchases which a hungry man might covet. When he confronted her, she screamed. Her son, Calum Campbell, Mac Iain Bhain, was near at hand. He had been travelling with his mother but fell behind for reasons of his own. When he came on the scene, there was a struggle in which he wrested a knife from Mac an t-Srònaich's hand. The Campbells kept the knife for many years as a souvenir, but, unfortunately, it was lost overboard from a fishing boat, and is now at the bottom of the Atlantic.

Calum, having survived his affray with a man regarded as a mass murderer, met his death in the Crimea by drinking water — from a well the Turks had poisoned. His father, Ian Ban, as I have heard the story, was one of the first to settle in the village of Arnol. He was reputedly descended, four generations back, from a man who had himself been a fugitive from justice — an Argyllshire youth who was accused of killing someone in a brawl in Glasgow College.

The warrant for the man lurking in the moors no longer exists. It was destroyed, I am told, during a spring cleaning in the Sheriff Clerk's office. The sort of spring cleaning which is really an act of historical vandalism.

Fortunately the text has been preserved, appropriately, by a policeman, but acting in a purely private capacity. Pursuing family history, as I am doing now.

A quarter of a century ago, a letter appeared in the *Stornoway Gazette* about Mac an t-Srònaich. It was signed "Iar-ogha Domhnuill 'c Neacail". No written evidence now exists as to the identity of the elusive great-grandson of Donald Nicolson, but there are phrases in the letter which, in some uncanny way, conjure up before me a Lewis policeman for whom I had a high regard.

The warrant from which he quotes is a curious document. Very unlegal in its phraseology. It is headed, "Proc. Fiscal v Bodach no Mondach or Fantom. A Moor Stalker."

A "Fantom"! That seems to be precisely what Mac an t-Srònaich was.

The warrant mentions no name although Mac an t-Srònaich's identity must have been well known to many people in Lewis. It mentions no specific crime committed either before Mac an t-Srònaich came to Lewis or while he was on the island.

The Procurator Fiscal's application to the Sheriff for a warrant says merely that he had received information "of there being a man lurking about the island of Lewis who is suspected of having committed some serious crime but for the present has evaded being brought to justice."

It goes on to say that he is "armed with dangerous weapons" and "puts the inhabitants of the island in fear for their lives." It also says they are afraid their sheep and cattle may be destroyed and their goods carried away, but there is no suggestion that any assault had taken place, or that anyone's stock or goods had been interfered with.

As the writer of the letter to the Gazette aptly comments, the person mentioned in the application for a warrant seems to be "the prototype of 'the man who's going about' of whom we hear now and again in the present day in the enlightened and civilised town of Stornoway, and who also appeared from time to time on the Lewis moors when I was a wee herd laddie."

The Procurator Fiscal in his application asked for authority to apprehend the "Fantom" to be given not only to the officers of the court and constables but "to any of the natives of the island."

The purpose of this is not at all clear. Was the threat so serious that the appointed representatives of the law had to be reinforced by vigilantes, or was the Fiscal, by inference, challenging the people of Lewis actually to produce the "Fantom" about whom they were making so much fuss?

In any event, when the Sheriff granted the warrant he did not include "the natives of the island". And there is no evidence that the warrant he issued was ever executed.

My own guess is that Mac an t-Srònaich was on the run for a much less serious crime than murder, and was being protected by his many influential relatives in Stornoway and rural Lewis, because of the savage sentences imposed in these days even for trivial offences.

Around 1820 a "young and handsome" woman was publicly flogged through the streets of Elgin, thrice within a fortnight, for some undisclosed offence. In 1823, two men who robbed a porter at the Caledonian Coach Office in Inverness were sentenced to death. The sentence was later commuted to transportation. In 1837 — four years after the warrant for the "Fantom" was issued — two men were sentenced, in Inverness, to transportation for life on a charge of forgery.

Any family with a "black sheep" on the run had good reason to shield him, whether they approved of his conduct or not.

11
Two Mysteries Remain

Piquancy is added to the story of Mac an t-Srònaich by the fact that one of his refuges was in the outbuildings of a manse.

Rev Robert Finlayson, a native of Clyth in Caithness, was one of the leaders of the evangelical revival in Lewis in the 19th century. He was known as the "John Bunyan of the North". When he was ordained at Knock in 1829, large numbers of people walked from Stornoway every night to attend his "parlour meetings". Every inch of space in the manse was occupied by worshippers on these occasions.

In 1831 he was translated to Lochs, and it is in the manse at Keose the "fantom" is said to have found succour. Finlayson's wife, Lilias Macaulay, was a first cousin of Mac an t-Srònaich.

If Mac an t-Srònaich had been the mass murderer of the Lewis tradition, butchering children in every peat bog in the island, it must have been a great embarrassment to an evangelical preacher to acknowledge him as a relative by marriage, and condone the furtive hospitality he received around the manse.

One story which has come to me, from the Carloway area, asserts that on one occasion the minister and the outlaw came to blows. The outlaw is said to have attacked the minister with a stone inside a stocking. In a variant of the story about his death-bed repentance for the murder of a child, the Carloway story says that, on the gallows, he expressed his regret for only two things — he had killed the child, and he hadn't killed the minister!

That story does not have the ring of truth, but it does encapsulate a truth — there must have been an uneasy relationship between the minister and his wife's mysterious cousin.

There is probably more substance in the traditions which have come down in two Lewis families which had connections with the manse at Keose.

"Iar-ogha Domhnuill 'c Neacail", be he policeman or no, claims that one of his great-grandaunts on the paternal side was a servant with the Finlaysons and supplied Mac an t-Srònaich with food and drink on many occasions.

Not long ago I had a letter from a very old friend and neighbour to tell me that her great-grandmother, Hannah Maciver, had been a nursemaid at Keose. One morning, when they were at family worship, she was terrified to see a black-visaged, unkempt man looking in the dining room window. It was well known in my informant's family that Mrs Finlayson was in the habit of putting out food for her cousin who was lurking in the Arnish Moor.

Oddly, the letter giving me this information was written by a Stornoway lady, in a train in Inverness station, and posted to me from Derbyshire. While it was being written, the writer looked up and saw me pass the carriage window, apparently hurrying out of the station. Actually I was going to the bookstall for a newspaper. I joined the same train, and travelled for something like six hundred miles with my informant and the letter, without us meeting up.

Apart altogether from the inconvenience of having a murderer, or a "fantom", haunt the purlieus of his manse, Robert Finlayson found his faith severely tried at Keose.

On a July afternoon in 1849, the minister's two sons, with a young cousin from Stornoway, and three local lads, set off for a fishing expedition in Loch Erisort. They had not returned by nightfall and, in the morning, a search revealed their upturned boat, aground on Tabhaigh. It was clear that the sheet had been tied when a squall struck them. A desperate attempt seems to have been made to cut it loose, but it was too late. All six were drowned.

Donald, the Finlayson's older boy, seems to have clambered on to the upturned boat and got his boots off. He then swam ashore. His palms were scratched and bruised in an unavailing effort to pull himself up the rocks. He was 17 and a very promising student.

His cousin, Donald Macaulay, was only 11. His body was taken back to Stornoway for burial. His father was a ship's captain, and that may give us a slender clue as to what became of Mac an t-Srònaich in the end of the day.

"Iar-ogha Domhnuill 'c Neacail" had a double link with the outlaw. While his great-grandaunt, on the paternal side, supplied the fugitive with food, his great-grandfather, on the maternal side, Donald Nicolson of Guershader, "shared the doubtful comfort and protection of an upturned boat at Sober Island" with Mac an t-Srònaich, on "his last night in Lewis".

Sober Island is on the wrong side of Stornoway Harbour for anyone joining a vessel legitimately. It would be a good jumping off point for someone being smuggled on board. It might well be that some of the outlaw's seafaring relatives were taking him discreetly, beyond the reach of the law.

Even if we accept that hypothesis, two mysteries remain. Why was he on the run in the first place, and why did a fugitive, who committed none of the atrocious crimes imputed to him, bulk so large in the Lewis tradition? The second of these is perhaps more difficult, and more interesting, than the first.

The offence for which an innkeeper's son was most likely to have fallen foul of the law was, surely, smuggling. It was rife in the Highlands around the time Mac an t-Srònaich flourished, and it was a crime condoned by the rich and influential as well as the poor. Perhaps more than the poor. After all, it was the well-to-do who drank the claret and the schnapps.

The *Inverness Courier* reports an affray near Muir of Ord in 1830 in which excisemen were shot at. One had his hat blown off, but he escaped serious injury. The excisemen made no attempt to pursue their assailants because they had no idea of their number.

A few years earlier there had been an even more serious clash between excisemen and smugglers in much the same area, in which a horse was killed and a man badly wounded. On that occasion it was not liquor that was being smuggled but salt, which was also subject to a heavy duty. The smugglers were making their way from the west coast to Inverness market, with a train of twenty laden pack horses.

The following year an illicit still was found at Abriachan, in a chamber hacked out of the rock which formed the foundations of a house. The smoke from the still was led into the chimney of the house.

In Grantown a number of women were fined for making and selling candles, illegally!

There is plenty of evidence that the Highlands was still resisting the tax laws of central government, and that the resisters had the weight of public opinion on their side.

A few years after Sheriff John Mackenzie signed the warrant for the arrest of the "Fantom" we know as Mac an t-Srònaich, his own nephew, Lewis Maciver of Gress, the uncrowned king of Lewis, was accused of smuggling. An accusation which resulted in a duel on Tong Sands which I will have occasion to refer to later, in another context.

Whether Mac an t-Srònaich was a smuggler or not, the evidence, such as it is, suggests that he committed no major crime in Lewis, certainly not murder. Why does he bulk so much larger than life in the Lewis legend?

My policeman friend suggests, a little cynically perhaps, that Mac an t-Srònaich was used as cover for deaths from exposure or accident, on the moor, arising from over indulgence. He cites the prevalance of the story about the man with the broken piggie, in support of his view.

Another friend, well qualified to make the point, suggests that Mac an t-Srònaich cast a long shadow because of the cultural vacuum which existed in Lewis at the time the "fantom" flourished.

The old paternalistic clan chiefs had become evicting lairds, with the result that the social fabric of the community was in disarray. The old easy-going tolerant church, which had embraced the whole community, had been replaced by a rigorous, evangelistic, eclectic regime which fenced off the great majority from the communion table: a division which is reflected in the fact that the great majority of Lewis people, to this day, are adherents rather than members of the church they attend, but accepted as such, as if the community was trying subconsciously to heal — or at least conceal — a stratification which was foreign to its egalitarian nature. The same ecclesiastical change proscribed many of the entertainments of the past, and belief in the supernatural was under attack both in the church and the schools.

This is an interesting theory, which suggests that there is an area of what one might call psychological history which requires study by some one better qualified than I am to reach conclusions. So much of history is concerned only with flotsam — the people and events which bob about on the surface, moved, not by their own dynamic as they believe, but by unseen currents far below, which should be our real subject matter.

Be that as it may, it is an amusing thought that my notorious relative Mac an t-Srònaich may have been nothing more than a surrogate for the *each uisge,* (the water horse,) the church had banished. But don't let us despise our ancestors for their credulity. We are just as credulous, but in a different way. Sometimes in the same way, for that matter.

It is not so many years since a group of airmen, using advanced technology in their daily work, saw a ghost on the Uig road, and took the matter seriously enough to report it formally to the police. They had seen the white figure of a woman, walking along the road before them in the dark, but suddenly she disappeared.

William Carrocher, now Head of Information Services with the BBC in London, was a reporter with me on the *Gazette* at the time. I told him, jokingly, that he had spoiled a good story, which might have run for weeks, by finding the explanation too quickly. As soon as he heard of the airmen's adventure, he had phoned the redoubtable Mrs Perrins of Lea and Perrins Sauces and of Garynahine. Yes! She was the ghost.

After dinner she had gone out for a breath of air, wearing a transparent raincoat over a white evening dress. When she saw the lights of an approaching car, she decided they might be poachers, and hid in the ditch to see what happened. The airman stopped and searched for her, but did not find her hiding place.

If we had as little to talk about, and as few distractions, in the 1960's, as Lewis people had in the 1830's, the police might have issued a warrant for the "fantom" of Betty Perrins, at the behest of the RAF.

A "fantom" we may meet again in a later volume of these reminiscences!

43

12
A Corsair from the Throat of Tunis

Whatever Mac an t-Srònaich may have been, the last of my auntie Jessie's trio, the Claw, was a hobo pure and simple. On one occasion a Stornoway lady, whose descendants were close neighbours and friends of mine, went to London to marry him. The Claw turned up at the wedding, very down at heel, and dressed in a paper suit!

Yes! A paper suit! That's what Jessie said, and who am I to doubt her, having twice proved her right?

On another occasion the Claw took a sour skate to America. Sour skate was a delicacy in Lewis in my youth. Well, perhaps not a delicacy. Let me say it was highly esteemed. The smell of the skate was so potent it had to be hung outside the house while it ripened, and it was eaten, according to report, not so much for its flavour as for its side effects. It was reputed to be an aphrodisiac, and was the subject of many sniggering adolescent tales.

Whether the Claw carried his skate for its flavour or its potency, I have no idea. My guess is that it was intended as a treat for some exiled Lewisman he hoped to meet at the end of the voyage. Long before then, however, the smell began to pervade the ship, and a worried captain had the holds turned out on deck. He was afraid his cargo had perished.

The Claw was close enough for Jessie to have known him herself, but he leads us into a gallery of seafaring men who survive now only as the memory of a memory, in my vague and fading recollection of Jessie's family reminiscences.

The Claw's father was known in the family as the Spaniard's Gash, because of a scar on his cheek. Whether he had sustained the wound on war service, as the nickname might imply, or whether he had quarrelled with the Spaniard in a pub ashore, I have no idea, and am not likely now to find out. Of more interest is the fact that his brother and brother-in-law were both seized by the press gang, and never heard of again.

This somewhat puzzles me. Here are two stories of the press gang in my own family, and yet I have always had the feeling that the press gang does not bulk so large in the Lewis tradition as it does, for instance, in Shetland. In Shetland the press gang has the place in the local demonology reserved for the Clearances in the Highlands and Islands. It may be that there is a more widespread tradition about the press gang in the west than I am aware of. I have been cut off from quite a lot in the island's past by the language barrier. But Donald Macdonald in his History of Lewis suggests another explanation. He states that, in 1807, the Admiralty decided to exempt fishermen on the West Coast of Scotland from the attentions of the press gang, provided that one man out of every six enlisted voluntarily in the service.

Donald's source is the Seaforth Muniments, and certainly in 1807 the Mackenzies, and other West Highland chiefly families, still had sufficient influence for the residents in their territories, be they clansmen or no, to accept "voluntary" enlistment on whatever scale the laird thought proper.

Some years before that, in 1801 to be precise, the *Naval Chronicle* referred to the service rendered to the navy by seafaring men from "the Western Scottish Islands or Hebrides". The arrangement referred to in the Seaforth papers in 1807 may well have had antecedents, or the lairds might have been busy doing their own pressing, to demonstrate their loyalty with other men's lives.

Discipline would not have been so severe in the merchant navy but the risks were just as great. There is a story in my own family of an encounter one of my relatives had with pirates on the North African Coast which makes the point, but gives it an unusual twist.

The Captain involved was John Mackenzie who, as I understand it, was my great grandfather's brother-in-law, and a grandson of Ruaraidh Mor who was tacksman at Brollum in Parc. It is, however, a little complicated, and confusing, because my grandfather and my great grandfather were both Roderick Morison, and each of them married a Mackenzie.

Whatever his precise relationship, Captain John was on a voyage to Naples as master of the *Freeland* — a Stornoway-owned vessel — when he had to put into Tunis for water. While in port he attended a Masonic dinner at which the Bey of Tunis and other potentates were present.

Shortly after he left port, a few days later, the vessel was becalmed. As it lay helpless, a corsair swept out of the Throat of Tunis and seized the ship. The crew were lined up, ready to walk the plank, when Capt John recognised his captor as one of the guests he had met at the Masonic dinner. He made the Masonic sign, and, in that way, saved both crew and cargo.

Many of the shipmasters of that generation seem to have been Freemasons, and a number of foreign shipmasters were admitted to the craft through Lodge Fortrose while their ships were in Stornoway. In the register of members one comes on names like John Knudston, Neils Von Der Hundd, and Toris Rasir Stein. Clearly Freemasonry meant a good deal to seafaring men, but while it is possible to understand the appearance of foreign shipmasters on the register of a Hebridean Lodge, one name has often puzzled me — William Lopson, surgeon, admitted to Lodge Fortrose in 1809.

Not long ago, quite out of the blue, I got the explanation, thanks to Iain Maciver, who is an assistant keeper in the National Library of Scotland, and both of whose parents were friends of mine at school and university.

Iain drew my attention to a passage in a book by Sir George Steuart Mackenzie describing his travels in Iceland in the summer of 1810. He had

45

as his guide a young native of Iceland, Olave Loptson, who was in practice as a surgeon in Stornoway.

Sir George explains that Loptson had been on a voyage from Iceland to Copenhagen when his vessel was forced to shelter in Stornoway Harbour. War had broken out, by that time, between Britain and Denmark and, instead of getting shelter, the crew and passengers, including Loptson, were detained as prisoners. Later Loptson was liberated, and, "having acquired some slight knowledge of medicine...in his native country", he "contrived to make himself useful to the people of Lewis."

Mackenzie's expedition to Iceland aroused great interest in the north of Scotland. Mrs Grant of Laggan says in one of her letters that people could speak of nothing else. She described Sir George as "a scientific Highland baronet", and visualised him piercing "the very midriff of Hecla", and coming home with "unheard of quantities of sulphur and crystals". The expedition was a follow-up to an earlier expedition by Sir Joseph Banks who visited Iceland before voyaging with Captain Cook to the South Seas. It was he who chose William Bligh to command the *Bounty* on her ill-fated voyage and so, indirectly, despatched one of my seafaring kinsmen to Tahiti and thence to a naval court martial.

We have a vivid portrait of Capt John Mackenzie of the *Freeland* in *Glimpses of Portrona,* written by his grand-nephew R. M. Stephen. A minor mystery surrounds it. Roddie Stephen describes two captains, under fictitious names, in the same chapter. So far as I know there is no one now alive who can say for sure which of the two is John Mackenzie. But there is some internal evidence which will enable us make a guess.

The two men are sharply contrasted and Roddie Stephen's portraits of them give us the flavour of Stornoway, a hundred years ago, when it was still deeply engaged in the carrying trade on all the oceans of the world.

Of one captain Stephen writes, "He was a fiery, overbearing, hoarse-voiced man, whose very face warned you that it would be dangerous to trifle with him. He was coarse enough, and his language when irritated was not fit for virgins and boys to hear.

"Yet he had withal a certain stateliness, and passed among us for a gentleman; he was rich enough to have his fling and hear little about it...He was a mighty man to drink whisky, without letting his legs or his brain tell the tale too plainly. Whether he could be said to have any religion I will not undertake to determine. Sunday differed from other days in that he had to do his drinking at home...

"If he was a pagan, he had at least some pagan virtues. He detested all pretence; he knew an honest man when he met one, and would respect him, and emphasised his respect, perhaps with an oath; and he himself acknowledged some rude quarter-deck decalogue."

Of the other captain, Stephen writes, "He could bear scrutiny. Not that he was a saint or a very fine and tender man. He had plainly a strong tincture of iron in his composition; he could be hard, and unjust, and unrelenting in his antipathies. His face, ruddy to the last, had sharp lines in it, and the mouth spoke of a stubborn, and perhaps narrow, resoluteness. But no one who knew him ever doubted that he was a man of antique mould, of sturdy honesty, and would never wittingly defraud, or malign, or deal a foul stroke.

"In his long frock-coat of fine broadcloth, with a corner of the red pocket handkerchief hanging out of its tail, he walked to church every Sunday afternoon with a firm, heavy step. It was characteristic of him that he adhered to the Establishment when most of his neighbours left it. He naturally took the side of cool moderation against anything like enthusiasm and stood by authority against popular attack or recalcitrance. His idea of civil and ecclesiastical government smacked of the quarter-deck...His old-fashioned collar, with its ample swathing of fine silk stock, held his head stiff as in a socket, and his whole body, though the years bowed it a little, was bravely borne...

"He had acquired what went among us for a modest fortune; but he often feared that it might not serve him till he got his final discharge. He victualled his house for the winter as he would his ship when putting forth on a voyage. He spoke of his outlay as disbursements, and kept acount of it accurately, as if he were still responsible to owners in Liverpool or London. His young friends, on their occasional visits home, were frequently disconcerted with awkward questions as to the price of beef or potatoes in the great cities. But his conversation was chiefly of the past.

"He dated events by his voyages; this happened when he was at Marseilles with the 'Scottish Thistle', that when he made his first voyage to Bahia with the 'Eliza Jermyn', and he could date some incident because he heard of it when lying at Leghorn in the 'Pearl.'"

Roddie Stephen describes his two captains as Captain David and Captain James. David was the hard drinker. James the moderate church-goer. In real life they were Captain John Mackenzie, Iain Mac Iain Mhic Ruraridh Mhoir, and Captain Donald Mackenzie, Domhnull Cubair. My guess is that Captain James is to be identified with Captain John Mackenzie. Stephen appears to have changed the names but kept the initials, James for John and David for Donald. Captain David is said to have "owned some vessels in Portrona (i.e. Stornoway) and had shares in prosperous companies." That, I know from other sources, was true of Domhnull Cubair but not of John Mackenzie.

Perhaps most conclusive of all, Stephen says he knew Captain David, "as a face one has seen occasionally at a window," but he writes of Captain James as a man he had "sat near". Clearly the man he sat near, and "sometimes surprised in deshabille", must have been his grand-uncle.

The manner in which the relationship between grand-uncle and grand-nephew came to be established in the first place is a story of its own.

13
Why Rory Shot the Sun

When the *Freeland* of Stornoway was boarded by pirates off the Tunisian coast, and the crew narrowly escaped being made to walk the plank, Capt. John Mackenzie's first mate was a young man from Boddam, near Peterhead, named George Stephen.

At the end of the voyage, perhaps influenced by the danger they had gone through, which must have drawn the two men pretty close together, the captain took the mate to Stornoway on a visit.

Stephen promptly fell in love with the Captain's niece by marriage, Catherine Morison, my grandaunt. According to family tradition Stephen was so deeply smitten, he departed somewhat from convention during the marriage service by offering the bride his hand with the words, "There's my hand, Kate, and you have my heart along with it!"

When he was absent from home, Donald Munro, the notorious factor, whose name is still anathema in Lewis a hundred years after his death, tried to get possession of Stephen's house, by harrying his young wife for the repayment of a debt for which Stephen, rather unwisely, had gone security. Munro went so far as to have my grandaunt thrown into prison, despite the fact that she was breast-feeding unweaned twins. The forced separation of mother and children caused an uproar in the town, and she was quickly released. But not quickly enough. The twins died, and she never recovered from her ordeal.

George Stephen was not a man to take things lying down. As soon as he got back to Stornoway, he raised an action in the Court of Session against Munro, and won it. It must have been the first occasion anyone stood up to the tyrant, who was eventually destroyed, in another court case, by the crofters of Bernera. A court case which is, oddly, neglected in popular accounts of "the crofters' war". Possibly because it was successful. Probably because it showed the effectiveness of constitutional methods, rather than the direct action beloved of those who exploit the Clearances for their own political purposes.

At one stage in his career, whether before or after his brush with Munro I cannot be sure, George Stephen was chief officer on the *Anne,* when she carried to the Behring Strait the first telegraph cable to connect the continents of Europe and Asia.

A few yards along the street from his home in Newton, lived Angus Macdonald who was, I think, a carpenter, on the *Great Eastern* when she laid the cable linking Europe and America. Wherever there was work to be done at sea in those days there were not only Lewismen but Newton men around!

I didn't know Angus Macdonald. He was before my time. But I knew his daughters well, and his son. His son was headmaster at Aird for many years, while the daughters, Tina and Annabella — as everyone knew them — sailed through the town like stately Spanish galleons. Magnificent women, who created something of a sensation in their old age by going to Rome on holiday and reporting on their return that they had "kissed the Pope's toe" — presumably they meant the statue of St Peter. In their youth they created an equal sensation by circling the royal yacht so closely in their rowing boat, when King Edward visited Stornoway, that they were able to peek through a port hole, and catch a glimpse of the monarch, naked in his bath.

On one occasion, in New York, George Stephen had a narrow escape when his ship foundered under him, before it had even sailed. The vessel was laden with iron for Spain.

Aptly, it was named the *Escape.*

More interestingly, it was Stornoway-owned. It belonged to Domhnull Cubair, one of the two captains I have mentioned. The fact that a vessel trading between USA and Spain should be owned in Stornoway underlines the point I have been making about the involvement of the port in the carrying trade of the world, in the middle years of last century, and the blow the local economy sustained when the big shipping lines took over.

George Stephen was also involved for some years in the palm oil trade, and his last voyage was to West Africa, on a vessel called the *Perilla* of which he was part-owner as well as master. My grandfather, his brother-in-law, sailed as mate.

While involved in this trade, Stephen contracted malaria, and, by the time the *Perilla* got to Africa, he was worn out with repeated bouts of fever. He was lying in his berth, a dying man, when they made their landfall.

"Did you shoot the sun, Rory?" he asked my grandfather.

"Yes", said Rory.

"Let me have the angle, and I'll work it out," said Stephen.

When he had completed his calculations he said, "Take soundings. I think we'll anchor here." And he did. He died next day, and was buried on the Calabar coast.

My grandfather brought the *Perilla* home, and when he died in 1917, well on in his nineties, there was an old-fashioned octant hanging in the shed behind the house, where he kept a great variety of carpenter's tools. I have no idea whether that was the instrument with which he "shot the sun", when his captain lay dying, but I kept it for many years as a reminder of the fact that, for at least three generations, every male relative on my mother's side of the family, of whom I have trace, with two exceptions, was a seafaring man. Five at least of them were drowned, or died at sea, without counting the two who were press-ganged, and disappeared. Eventually I presented the octant to the Lewis museum as a relic of an important era in the history of the island.

Although George Stephen was an incomer, his son, Rev R. M. Stephen, became, in a sense, the historian of the town, or at least the historian of the period in the history of the town which was within recall when he was a boy. His daughter married the representative of another seafaring family which came into Lewis and settled down, greatly enriching the local tradition.

Peter Pope was a Stornowegian, born and raised in the town, but the family had come to Lewis from the south coast of England, via Rothesay. In his day Peter was one of the outstanding captains in a town of colourful characters. Powerfully built, fiery and courageous.

During the American civil war he was first officer on a Liverpool clipper barque engaged in running the blockade, taking much needed goods into the Southern states, and cotton back for the Lancashire mills. On one occasion they were captured and seized as a prize of war. Most of the crew were removed, but the Captain, the first officer, the carpenter, bosun and cook were kept on board. When their captors broached the rum, Peter and his companions seized their chance, overpowered their captors, and battened them down in the f'c'sle.

The five of them then sailed the ship back to Liverpool, no mean achievement.

It is interesting to recall that a Stornoway man, in the person of Peter Pope, was First Officer, and then master, of one of the first four-masted full-rigged ships ever built. He left Calcutta with her just before the Franco-Prussian war broke out in 1870, carrying a cargo of jute and some passengers for Dundee. When they reached the English channel they were told that Paris had fallen and the war was over. "What war?" they asked blankly. There was no radio in those days. A ship at sea was in a world of its own. The whole war had been fought while they were out of touch.

Another of his ships, the *Kenilworth* was badly strained by the monsoon winds in the Indian ocean and began to leak. When it got to Liverpool, repairs were carried out and the vessel was sold to some Americans. The B.O.T., however, refused to issue a certificate of seaworthiness.

Peter Pope nevertheless signed on a crew, and set off for Galveston, Texas, in mid-winter, with hurricane weather in the Atlantic. The vessel sprung a leak, and the pumps had to be manned, 24 hours a day. The crew tried to lighten the task, as sailors did in those days, by singing as they worked, their favourite song being the topical, "Marching Through Georgia." They reached Galveston safely. When he made that exacting voyage, Peter Pope was only 28.

Many years later his son, Willie, who figures in my earlier books, was lying in his bunk reading, on board the large steamship of which he was chief engineer. Another engineer came into his cabin and gave him a bundle of newspapers he had just received from home. One of them was a

Liverpool paper which was running a series of articles by a retired ship's captain. Willie read them with professional interest.

He was half-way through an account of a desperate voyage across the Atlantic, in mid-winter, in which the crew had been held together by the courage of their captain, before Willie realised he was reading about his own father. A father he had never seen, because Peter Pope was washed overboard, during a hurricane off the Horn, in the year his son was born!

The writer of the reminiscences had been an apprentice on the *Kenilworth*. Willie was later able to contact him in Nova Scotia and get a first-hand account of his father's achievement.

14
Spanish Coins in a Secret Drawer

The attempt by pirates to seize the *Freeland* of Stornoway took place many hundreds of miles from Lewis, but there was an occasion, not very many years before, when pirates actually landed in Lewis. Not by choice, but by misadventure! They turned out to be the last pirates publicly executed in Scotland, and I still have in my possession two silver coins which formed part of their hoard.

The coins had been in the possession of my uncle, Roddie. I knew he had them because he showed them to me on more than one occasion. But, when he died, I could not find them. I was afraid that Anna, his sister, who was beginning to get a little absent-minded, might have mistaken them for British money, and used them to pay some unsuspecting vanman or shopkeeper. Some time later my sister-in-law, Sheila Macleod, moved into the Newton house to look after my aunt, and her husband came on the coins, in a secret drawer, in my uncle's desk, which I had missed. They were wrapped in a piece of paper recording that they had been given to him by the Misses Millar, two elderly spinsters whom he used to visit whenever he was in Edinburgh.

Shortly after they gave them to him, they died of gas poisoning, in a boarding house in Helensburgh, where they had gone for a short holiday. They were well over ninety then, and had been in the habit of getting up, in the middle of the night, to make themselves a cup of tea. Apparently they did not turn the gas off properly, and in the morning they were dead in bed. They were descendants of Flora Macdonald, and among their treasures was a lock of Prince Charlie's hair.

The Misses Millar belonged to Stornoway, and were very close friends, if not relatives, of my uncle. Their grandfather was the doctor in Lewis when the pirates were arrested. He figures, too, in the tradition about the Old Soldiers of Uig, mentioned in an earlier book.

Iain MacThormoid of Crowlista who, as I have told, interrupted the minister's prayer because he praised the Turks, who had taken him prisoner and maltreated him, had a wound on his cheek which never healed. It required periodic attention from the doctor, and the old soldier is reputed to have said to Dr Millar, on one occasion, in Gaelic, "I have been to Lower Egypt, and I have been to Upper Egypt, I have travelled where I have travelled, but I never met a man to equal you." For many years Millar was the only doctor in Lewis. He was almost worshipped.

The pirates' coins were common enough in Stornoway at one time, but, so far as I know, Dr Millar was the only person sufficiently interested to preserve a few, and hand them on. They were Spanish "hard dollars", of different sizes and denominations.

After the discovery of the pirates' cache, the dollars were carried in sacks, by the crofters, from the beach at Swordale, where the pirates had hidden them, to a barn at Swordale Farm. From there they were taken in carts to Stornoway. Many of the dollars went missing in transit, and it was said that, for years afterwards, you could not cash a £1 note in Stornoway without getting Spanish money in the change.

So far as Lewis is concerned, the story of the pirates began on a Sunday evening, in July 1821, when the tenants of the tacksman at Tolsta Farm saw a wreck some distance from the shore.

Lewis was not then as strictly Sabbatarian as it afterwards became. Indeed, it was three years after the year of the pirates that the great religious revival in Uig began, under the ministry of Rev Alexander Macleod.

Not being constrained by the day of the week, the Tolsta crofters launched a boat and went to see what they could salvage from the wreck. They found she was a copper-bottomed schooner, water-logged and on her beam ends. There was no sign of the crew. The Tolsta men got a rope, and tried to take the vessel to a place of safety but a gale blew up, and they had to desist. In the morning the vessel was in a cove near Tolsta Head. She had broken in the gale, and pipes of sweet oil, bales of paper, barrels of beeswax, jars of olives and bags of aniseed were floating in all directions. There was nothing to indicate the identity of the vessel, or what had happened to her.

The tacksman sent a messenger to Stornoway, on the Monday evening, to tell the Receiver of Wreck. It is interesting to speculate why he delayed for more than a day in making his report. Had he got scruples about Sabbath travelling which the crofters at that time did not share? Or was he hoping to get some quiet pickings before the authorities intervened? Or was he just philanthropically giving the crofters their chance? We'll never know.

The Receiver of Wreck was getting ready to set off for Tolsta, on the Tuesday morning, when his colleague, Roderick Maciver, the Surveyor of Customs, gave him information which sent him scurrying instead to Swordale.

At the weekend Maciver had heard reports of a strange vessel off the coast, near Stornoway. He suspected it might be a smuggler. Smuggling was rife in the Western Isles. The government stationed Capt Oliver with a revenue cutter on the coast to try to suppress it. In 1827, just six years later, the *Inverness Courier* reported that Capt Oliver had at last succeeded in suppressing smuggling in the Western Isles, with the result that the largest consignment of legal whisky in local history was in process of being shipped from Glasgow to Stornoway. Capt Oliver was stationed in the

Minch for a considerable period. It is after him Oliver's Brae near Stornoway is called.

In view of his suspicions, Maciver sent a boat out with four men, to look for the strange vessel. He himself followed, shortly afterwards, accompanied by his elder son. They found no trace of the vessel which had been reported to them, but saw a large fishing boat, ashore at Swordale, and six men, sheltering in an improvised tent on the beach.

One of the men told Maciver that he was George Sadwell, mate of the brig *Betsy* of New York, outward bound with a cargo of tobacco and cotton. The *Betsy,* he said, was lost off Barra Head. The Captain and he had quarrelled, with the result that the Captain had set off with five men in one boat to try to reach Liverpool, while he had taken the rest of the crew in another boat, to try to reach the Scottish mainland. They had been driven ashore at Swordale by contrary winds. The *Betsy,* added Sadwell, with a nice imaginative touch, had belonged to his father, hence, presumably, the friction between him and the Captain.

At that stage Maciver had no reason to disbelieve the story. He had no knowledge of the wreck at Tolsta with its cargo of sweet oil, olives and beeswax. With his mind still on smuggling, he searched their belongings. He found no contraband. But in each of the sea chests there was a surprising number of Spanish dollars.

15
The Cabin Boy's Story

The Surveyor of Customs was puzzled when he found the Spanish dollars in the sea chests of the "shipwrecked" crew. He decided to return to Stornoway, probably for consultation, but left two of his boatmen to keep a discreet eye on the crew of the *Betsy.*

He had only gone a hundred yards when the cabin boy, a Maltese, came panting after him to say that the vessel was not the *Betsy* at all. The Mate had murdered the Captain and taken possession of the ship. The helmsman, a Scot named Paterson, had also been killed. At that point Maciver sent two more boatmen back to watch. He told them to "keep all the country people that might come to the spot", as reinforcements. If the seamen attempted to escape, they were to stave the boat and secure the seaman with cord.

When he got to the top of the cliff Maciver paused to examine the cabin boy more closely. His name was Andrew Camelier, and, although he was only 18, he had been four years at sea. The *Betsy,* he said, was a schooner belonging to Gibraltar but, oddly, he could not remember its real name. He did remember the name of the Scottish captain — Thomas Johnston. The vessel had sailed from Malta but stopped at Gibraltar, where they took on board a new crew consisting of six men, in addition to himself and the captain. They were Peter Heaman, the mate, who now called himself Sadwell. Francois Gautier, the cook, a Frenchman. Three Scots — James Paterson, Peter Smith and Robert Strachan — and Johanna Dhura, also referred to as John Hard or Lawrence, "a Portugese who calls himself an Italian from Leghorn."

At Gibraltar they took on board a cargo of oil, olives, raisins, beeswax, paper and a little silk, for the Brazils, but he did not know which port they were bound for. The last of the cargo to come aboard was eight barrels of dollars, six large and two small, which were taken from the shore in the afternoon. The vessel sailed on the morning tide.

When they were about a fortnight at sea, the Cabin Boy continued, Peter Smith, who was in the mate's watch, cut his leg and had to stay below. The French cook took his place on watch. On the sixteenth or seventeenth day at sea, Camelier was wakened by a shot. He slept in the captain's cabin, head to head, with only a plank between them. He thought the shot had been fired into the captain's bed. It was dark when he went on deck. The first thing he saw was the mate attacking Paterson with the butt end of a musket. The captain then came on deck, holding his head, which was bleeding. The cook attacked him with a musket.

The mate called the sailors from the f'c'sle to come on deck, but, when they appeared, he only let one of them up — Johanna Dhura. The mate, who had an axe in his hand, ordered the two surviving Scots, Strachan and Smith, to go below again. The mate then ordered Camelier and Dhura to help heave the bodies of the captain and Paterson overboard. Paterson was dead, but Camelier did not think the captain was. They tied stones to his body before they threw him out. Camelier said he was crying, but helped the others, under duress.

In the morning, the mate nailed down the hatch on Smith and Strachan, and lit a fire in the cabin, which was next the f'c'sle, with wood from one of the water barrels, some powder and tar. Camelier was ordered to seal up all the crevices in the cabin with a paste of flour and water, and to bore holes in the bulkhead, so that the smoke would seep into the f'c'sle where the two Scots were held prisoner.

It is not clear whether the intention was to smother Smith and Strachan, or just to intimidate them, but the fire was kept burning from the morning of one day until the morning of the next, and Camelier overheard the mate and cook speculating whether the Scots were likely to be dead. On the second day, they opened the hatches and found them alive but dejected. They were not allowed on deck but were given some bread. The hatches were fastened down again. On the third morning, Dhura pled with the mate and cook to let the others up, and eventually they were released, after they had kissed the Bible, and sworn they would never tell what happened.

The casks of dollars were then taken on deck and broached.

Some of the dollars were in bags, and they made more bags to take the rest. They hid the bags behind the bulwarks. The mate took charge as captain. The cook became mate. They set course for Scotland.

The mate, with Strachan and Smith, went ashore in Barra and bought a fishing boat which they took on board. They loaded the dollars into the fishing boat and sailed towards Stornoway.

When they were off the Lewis coast, they scuttled the schooner by knocking holes in the bottom with a crowbar, and tried to reach the mainland in the fishing boat. Contrary winds drove them ashore at Swordale. The fishing boat was damaged when they beached, so they hauled it up, and built a tent over it to give themselves shelter. They hid the bulk of the money below the stones on the beach.

The only point at which Camelier's story about the unnamed schooner from Gibraltar tallied with "Sadwell's" story about the brig *Betsy* from New York, was that after the vessel sunk — or they thought it had sunk — the crew had attempted to land on the mainland of Scotland, but were driven to Lewis by contrary winds.

A short time later, Camelier's story was fully confirmed. The Tolsta wreck was identified as the *Jane* of Gibraltar, and, a search of the beach at Swordale revealed a hoard of dollars, hidden beneath the stones, precisely as he had said.

16
Beeswax by the Creelful

Heaman and Gautier, the ringleaders, were arrested for piracy and murder. They were tried, before the High Court of Admiralty in Edinburgh, in November 1821. They attempted to blame the other members of the crew for the crime, but their evidence did not shake the cabin boy's story, although it added some colour to it.

Heaman tried to make out that the 18 year old cabin boy had a feud with the captain, and was the most bloodthirsty of them all. When Camelier threw the captain's body overboard, said Heaman, he shouted, "There you go to hell, you bugger. You will never plague me more!" A remark — or its French equivalent — more likely to have been made by Gautier, the cook, who was forever in trouble with the captain because his pans were greasy.

Maintaining that he was no more in charge of the ship than the rest of them, after the mutiny, Heaman said he often found it necessary to take in the jib himself, or even swab down the decks, because the others refused to do so, "while they were amusing themselves with the dollars."

There may be an element of truth in the story. The other members of the crew are not likely to have taken kindly to Heaman's captaincy, whether they were act and part in the piracy with him or not.

Gautier, who described himself as a native of Harve-de-Grace, aged 23, said he did not understand the language of the rest of the crew, and did not hear any conversation about killing the captain or seizing the ship. Except, he added, in a complete giveaway, that it was jocularly mentioned that, if they could lay their hands on the money, they would all be made men of fortune.

How did he hear that if he did not know the language? And how could he detect that it was said jocularly?

Even more significantly, he revealed that all the crew, except the captain and the cabin boy, had previously been shipmates on the *Araquebassa,* and that, even if he could not speak English, his fellow conspirator, Heaman, could speak French.

When Gautier was first examined, before four Justices of the Peace in Stornoway, James Reid acted as interpreter. Reid had acquired his French in Lower Canada where he had been employed by the North West Fur Trading Company, through the influence of Sir Alexander Mackenzie, the explorer, who was a native of Stornoway, and a relative of the Reids by marriage.

John Reid, presumably James Reid's father or brother, who was a

Collector of Customs in Stornoway, figures in an incident connected with the Selkirk Settlers which is described by Prof Bumsted in his book *The People's Clearance,* and which is also used by Frederick Niven, the Glasgow-Canadian author, in his novel *Mine Inheritance.* The best account of the incident is to be found in the journal of John Macleod, a Lewisman from the village of Garrabost, who travelled to Hudson Bay with the settlers. He tells how the feud between the two great Canadian fur companies was fought out in the streets of Stornoway, showing how close the link was between Lewis and Canada when James Reid was learning French in Quebec.

Equally interesting is the fact that the official record at the interrogation of the mutineers was taken by Roderick Mackenzie, great-grandfather of Agnes Mure Mackenzie, the historian.

Evander Maciver, author of the rather egregiously titled *Memoirs of a Highland Gentleman,* gives a short account of the seizure of the *Jane* in his book. He was a schoolboy in Stornoway when the pirates landed, and saw the arrival at the Customs House — then part of a private dwelling — of several carts, loaded with silver dollars.

"The whole people of Stornoway, old and young, male and female," he says, turned out to see "such a wonderful and rare sight as cartloads of silver in the streets of the town."

He also remembered seeing beeswax from the *Jane* being sold though the streets by a woman who had it in a creel.

The sale of beeswax by a woman with a creel might not have been a very unusual sight on the streets of Stornoway in those days, although the source of the produce was normally more conventional. Osgood Mackenzie records that, when he was young, bees were so plentiful in Lewis the boys were able to collect large quantities of honey, which they drained from the combs into glass bottles and sold at the Stornoway markets. Hunting for wild bees was one of the great ploys of the boys in the autumn, he adds, "but no one thinks of it nowadays."

Even in the sixties (of last century!), he adds, his grieve used to complain that the harvest was frequently interrupted, because the men laid down their scythes to raid bees' nests in the grass, and then complained that they could not resume because they were pursued by angry bees.

Some years after he saw the women with the creel of beeswax in Stornoway, Evander Maciver was sent to school in Edinburgh. He took with him several Spanish dollars from the *Jane.* How he acquired them is not revealed! He sold them to a silversmith on the North Bridge for 3/10 each.

Although he was just a schoolboy at the time of the mutiny, Evander Maciver was well placed to know the facts. His granduncle, John Mackenzie, was Sheriff Substitute. His father, Lewis Maciver, being a farmer near where the *Jane* came ashore, and a shipowner in Stornoway, was also well placed to know the facts. Even more directly involved was Evander Maciver's grandfather, James Robertson, who was Collector of

Customs at Stornoway, and one of the JP's who conducted the interrogation. Evander was staying in his grandfather's house at the time, while attending school in Stornoway.

Both James Robertson and Lewis Maciver feature in my book *Surprise Island,* in connection with the story of Mary Carn whose brother was the first Surveyor General of India. It was James Robertson who went to London, after the Surveyor General's death, to take home to his sister a fortune of £30,000, the equivalent in modern money of more than three quarters of a million pounds.

Lewis Maciver was the uncrowned king of Lewis in his day. The toast to "the chief of the Macivers", at Mary Carn's funeral, was probably intended for him, perhaps with a gentle hint of mockery in the adulation.

It is a tradition in the island, perhaps again with the same gentle hint of mockery, that, when King William died in 1837, some of the old folk seriously believed that "Louis" would succeed him, because they were known to have been friendly when the king visited Stornoway as a young officer on board a man-of-war.

The future king got into some sailorly scrapes ashore, with considerable assistance from the locals.

More than twenty years after the incident of the *Jane,* Lewis Maciver took part in the last duel fought in Scotland, of which I first heard at our dinner table when my father read one of Johnny Anderson's "sugar bag" letters from Edinburgh*.

His opponent was a Collector of Customs named Macleay, who was indiscreet enough to accuse Maciver, in public, of smuggling.

The accusation suggests that the *Inverness Courier* was a little premature in reporting in 1827 that Capt Oliver had at last succeeded in stamping out smuggling in the Western Isles.

The sequel to Macleay's accusation, reinforces the point.

*The story of the "sugar bag" letters is told in *The Hub of My Universe.*

17
Duel at Tong Sands

Macleay's allegation that Lewis Maciver was a smuggler was specially piquant because Maciver was married to a daughter of Macleay's predecessor as Collector of Customs.

There were two distilleries in the island then, and a great many illicit stills, but even so, there was a brisk trade with the Faroes in cheap Danish schnapps. It may well be that Capt. Oliver suppressed the activities of vessels engaged in smuggling pure and simple, but was unable to suppress the activities of those, like Lewis Maciver, who were engaged in legitimate trade, and had the opportunity of taking in a little illicit schnapps, or claret, in the by-going for their own personal use.

In any event Maciver resented the imputation, and challenged Macleay to a duel. The two men were so angry they set off for Tong sands straightaway, to fight it out, without even waiting to get seconds.

The site they chose for the duel was a field, a little to the west of Goathill Farm, close to the sands.

It would be interesting to know how they proceeded to the chosen spot. Did they walk side by side, in surly silence? Did they keep up the argument and exchange of abuse? Or did they walk discreetly, a little distance from each other? They must have maintained some line of communication because, on their way, they met a tailor named Mackenzie, and pressed him into service, to hold their jackets and give the signal to fire.

The duel took place. The tailor fulfilled his function. The assailants both missed. Whereupon Macleay apologised, and Maciver took him home for a dram.

I wonder did they have whisky from one of the two distilleries, or was it smuggled schnapps?

The Procurator Fiscal at the time was Donald Munro. He had recently arrived in Lewis from Edinburgh, and presumably had not had time to establish the unpleasant reputation he later acquired, but, even then, he showed his penchant for trying to make trouble.

He got to hear of the duel. Took a statement from the tailor, discovered some people who had heard the shots, although they had not seen the duel, and prepared charges against the duellists.

He was infuriated when the papers were sent back to him from Crown Office with instructions that there should be no proceedings. The cause of his anger was probably less an interest in abstract justice than the fact that, at that time, the Fiscal got no salary. He got a fee for each successful prosecution.

Anderson adds that this practice continued for another thirty years or so. When it was abandoned there was such a dramatic drop in the number of prosecutions the gaol fell into disuse, and was finally sold to the County Council for £25, although it cost £1200 to build.

The gaol was built in 1832 and was still in use in my granny's day. She told me once that it was a high building, on the corner of Cromwell Street and North Beach, where Donald Macaulay had a draper's shop in my boyhood, and which is now the Town House cafe.

It seems to have been an oddly-designed building. According to my granny, there was a shop on the ground floor, the prison on the first floor, and a school in the attic! There was also a scolding-bridle fixed to the wall, but my granny did not say whether she had ever seen it in use.

There was no gaol in Stornoway, however, when the mutineers of the *Jane* were arrested in 1821. They were incarcerated in an hotel.

There was no procurator fiscal in Stornoway either at that time, although there was one a decade or so later when the warrant was issued for the "Bodach no Mondach or Fantom" I have presumed to be Mac an t-Srònaich. Presumably governments in the earlier period were not deeply concerned about the suppression of crime in the islands — except when it affected the revenue, or threatened the safety of the realm.

There was a Sheriff-substitute responsible for Lewis in 1821, — Evander Maciver's granduncle — but, at the time the mutineers came ashore, he was at his farm near Gairloch, and the four local justices were left to handle the affair as well as they could.

Eventually the mutineers were brought to trial in Edinburgh, and an account of the hearing was published by Alexander Stuart, clerk to the court. It was through this account I first heard of the *Jane,* long before the Millar sisters gave the silver coins to my uncle. I was just a youngster at the time, and I was spending the evening with my cousin Stephen MacLean. His brother, Peter, and their father, were discussing the mutiny. Peter had got a copy of the report of the trial from "Ballishan" Ranger, who was then working in the Estate office. His father was Sam Ranger, painter and Bailie. "Ballishan", in turn, as I remember it, had borrowed the report from Johnny Dol, who worked in a local solicitor's office, from which presumably it had come.

Many years later I was able to trace and buy a copy for myself. It may well have been the same one, but if so it had passed through several hands in the interval.

I also have a little pamphlet containing the text of a lecture on the *Jane* given by Johnny Anderson to raise funds for Stornoway's first Town Hall. I don't think giving public lectures, even on such an exciting subject would be a very effective way of raising funds today, but Anderson filled the hall.

He put forward the interesting theory that the dollars, which seem to have been shipped clandestinely, were intended to finance one side, or the other, in the war of liberation then being waged in Brazil. All that emerged at the trial, however, was that the *Jane* belonged to Moses Levy of

Gibraltar; that the cargo was insured in London through Abraham Levy Bensusan, "who was sworn solemnly on the Old Testament according to the rite of the Jewish religion"; that the voyage was insured from Gibraltar "to Bahia and all or any other port or place in the Brazils" and that Levy's office, in Gibraltar, was "in a small street, on the left hand, after entering the gate, about two hundred yards, and up one stair."

Which sounds the sort of place where dark deeds might be hatched.

18
Who was Captain Delano?

The trial of the mutineers of the *Jane* aroused great public interest, not only because of the nature of the offence, but because of the legal issues it raised. Some of them remarkably similar to the problems raised in our own day by the hi-jacking of planes.

The point was well put by the Lord Advocate to the jury. "It is to the punishment of offences committed in Scotland that the attention of juries in Scotland is demanded" he said. "But here, you see, we are called on to judge in a case which occurred many thousand miles distant from the nearest corner of this kingdom. You are called on to judge of a crime committed in a vessel not belonging to this country, or in any way connected with it. You are to judge as to persons not owing allegiance to this country, yet brought here to be tried. Such, however, is the jurisdiction of this court. Were jurisdiction confined to the place where the vessel belonged, or the individuals were domiciled, the offenders would take care to avoid such spots, and it would be impossible to punish their guilt.

"A shipmaster and his crew, a class of men who hold no high rank in society, however respectable they may be as individuals, are entrusted with immense property, and have the means of carrying it where they choose. They have on the one hand the temptation of riches, and an end of all their labour, and by an opposite course, merely their hard-earned wages and their character."

The jury were no doubt helped to a decision by Heaman's behaviour when he saw Camelier approach the Customs Officers, and by the fact that both he and Gautier were in possession of clothing and other articles which had belonged to the murdered captain.

The vital evidence at the trial in Edinburgh was given by John Murray, sub-tenant in Melbost, and great-grandfather of Dr Donald Murray, the first M.P. for the Western Isles, whose funeral, confusedly recalled in a dream helped to start me off on the writing of this series of books.

Murray, as his evidence showed, had a good command of English but he was examined in Gaelic, so that three languages, and two interpreters, were used at the trial.

Although, at the preliminary investigation in Stornoway, the Canadian French of James Reid had sufficed, the authorities took no chance in Edinburgh. Gabriel Surenne, a Frenchman teaching in the city, was sworn as interpreter. His task was to explain to Gautier everything that was said in court.

The Gaelic interpreter, whose task was simpler, was Gilbert MacDonald, also a teacher in Edinburgh.

Murray told the Court he was standing on the beach near Heaman when Camelier made his dash after Maciver, the Collector of Customs. Heaman immediately sent two men after the boy, remarking that he was very foolish, and did not care what he said or did at times. Then Heaman went in search of the boy himself, and came back in a state of great perturbation, having thrown off all his clothes in the chase, except his trousers and drawers.

The discarded articles included the captain's watch, and among the productions at the trial were a variety of other items belonging to the captain found in Heaman's or Gautier's possession.

Among them were "three muslin neckcloths, marked T.J. (the captain's name was Thomas Johnston); two muskets and a pistol; a silver watch with the name Wm Simpson, London on the dial plate; two pairs of cotton trousers, a striped cotton waistcoat, a striped cotton jacket, a green coat, a red and white muslin half handkerchief, a blue watchcoat; a book entitled *Trial of Captain Delano for Piracy;* a trunk with a canvas cover, a trunk with a calfskin cover; two plain white linen shirts, three pairs of short white cotton stockings, a pair of braces and two coarse hand towels."

Dress the captain, in imagination, in that wardrobe, and you have an idea of what our seagoing ancestors looked like a hundred and sixty years ago.

No explanation was given in Court about *The Trial of Captain Delano for Piracy.* The fact that the book belonged to the murdered captain is ironic, although I prefer not to believe that he had any piratical intentions himself, despite Heaman's allegation that, just before the *Jane* sailed, Gautier and the Portugese took their clothes on deck and said they wished to go ashore again, at which the captain called them "damned fools", and said they "didn't know when to do themselves good," adding "I mean to do some good for myself this voyage."

Whether the captain intended to turn pirate or not was irrelevant to the question the jury had to answer. They returned a verdict of guilty, and the Lord Advocate asked for a salutary sentence such as would "give security to the commerce of the world."

The judge, having told the prisoners that "to the misguided and penitent offender the door of mercy is sometimes opened, but against the pirate and murderer it will be for ever shut," sentenced them to be taken to the Tolbooth of Edinburgh therein to be detained, and to be fed on bread and water only, until the second Wednesday in January, when they were to be "taken forth of the said Tolbooth to the sands of Leith, within floodmark, and then and there hanged by the neck, upon a gibbet, by the hands of the common executioner, until they be dead, and their bodies thereafter to be delivered to Dr Alexander Munro, Professor of Anatomy in the University of Edinburgh, to be by him publicly dissected and anatomised."

The reference to the disposal of the criminals' bodies is a grisly reminder that that was the era of the body-snatchers or "resurrectionists", during which guard had to be mounted over graveyards in Scotland, or elaborate iron structures, called mortsafes, erected over graves, to prevent bodies being stolen after burial, and sold to the surgeons in the universities.

It was just four years earlier that William Burke, an Irish navvy, arrived in Edinburgh, and just eight years later that he was convicted, on the evidence of his accomplice, Hare, of having murdered fifteen people so that he could sell their bodies to Dr Knox, an anatomist in Edinburgh University, for prices ranging from £8 to £14.

Whatever happened to their bodies afterwards, the *Glasgow Herald* reported, at the time, that the prisoners were "respectable looking men." Heaman's countenance in particular was said to be of a "very superior cast". "They received the announcement of their melancholy fate with the greatest composure and bowed respectfully to the Court."

Two months later there was a great crowd in the streets when the two prisoners set out for the sands at Leith, accompanied by four bailies in carriages, and a detachment of Dragoon Guards. Heaman stood throughout the journey, bowing occasionally to the crowd.

When the procession arrived at the foot of Leith Walk they were joined by the magistrates of Leith. The combined party arrive at the scaffold about half past ten o'clock, and a considerable time was spent in prayer. There were three clergymen present, one of them a Catholic.

Rev Dr Campbell, came to the front of the scaffold and announced that Heaman acknowledged the justice of the sentence passed on him.

Heaman thereafter addressed the crowd, and corroborated the statement.

"The scaffold", reported the *Herald,* "was erected at the bottom of Constitution Street, immediately in the centre of the road, so that the whole proceedings could be seen a great way up the street. Everything passed off quietly."

To the involvement of Lewis in these events two silver coins hanging on my wall still bear mute testimony.

19
Lightning Strikes Twice

When I wrote about James Robertson, the Collector of Customs, in my last book, in connection with Mary Carn's legacy, and even here, in connection with the mutiny on the *Jane,* I had no idea who he was, beyond the fact that he was an incomer to Lewis.

Quite by chance, when looking for other things, I stumbled on the fact that his Stornoway-born son was a midshipman on the *Victory,* standing close to Nelson when he was killed, at the battle of Trafalgar, and that the Collector's father was a preacher well known in what one might describe, without disrespect, as the ecclesiastical folklore of the Highlands.

The father was Rev James Robertson, minister of Lochbroom, known generally as the *Ministear Laidir* — the strong minister. He earned the nickname on Oct 10th 1742 when Fearn church, in which he was preaching, was struck by lightning. The roof collapsed. Forty-two people were killed. Many more were injured. Robertson cleared the debris from one of the doorways and supported the lintel with his shoulder, enabling many to escape, including the frail old minister he had succeeded at Lochbroom.

Fearn Church was a very ancient building. It was part of an Abbey restored for use as a parish church. It had been struck by lightning once before, metaphorically speaking, when, in 1527, Patrick Hamilton, the abbot, introduced the doctrines of Luther to Scotland. He became the first — and one of comparatively few — native-born Protestant Scots to be burned at the stake as a heretic. As many leading Catholics recognised at the time, his martyrdom merely gave impetus to his cause. In the popular aphorism of the day, the reek of the fire in which he burned infected as many as it blew upon.

Governments never seem to learn that, in the dynamics of ideology, as in the dynamics of the physical world, action and reaction are equal and opposite. Repression does not produce uniformity but rebellion.

Two hundred years after Patrick Hamilton's death, the *Ministear Laidir* was singed by the dying embers of the same fire. Despite the halo of hero-worship which surrounded him, because of his extraordinary feat, he came into violent conflict with many of his parishioners, at the time of the Forty-Five. A strong supporter of the Hanoverian government, and a confidant of the Duke of Cumberland, he had his manse ransacked by Jacobites, looking for evidence against him. He was also arrested by Jacobite troops on the suspicion, which as it happened was well-founded, that he had passed a vital message from one group of the Hanoverian army to another. When cross-examination failed to break him down, his captors taunted him by asking him to drink a health to Prince Charlie. When he refused, they tried to trap him into an indiscretion by giving him the opportunity of drinking a toast to King George. He refused to drink toasts to anyone, and was released.

Many years later, one of his parishioners confessed, on his death bed, that he had thrust a loaded musket through the manse window, with the intention of shooting the minister. At the last minute he recoiled from committing murder, but he never forgave the minister for supporting the Hanoverians.

Robertson was not alone, among Highlanders, in welcoming Cumberland's victory at Culloden. We see the Jacobite rebellion through a haze of romance. We tend to look on Culloden as a victory of the English over the Scots, or the Lowlands over the Highlands, or, at least, of an Anglicising (or Germanising) central government over an indigenous, idyllic Highland civilisation. Just about twenty years ago, Inverness Choral Society was split when a prominent member refused to sing in *Judas Maccabeus* because Handel had dedicated it to Cumberland. The Butcher casts a long shadow.

The story of an individual at the centre of the conflict, like Rev James Roberston, reminds us that there were Highlanders on both sides. Many, even of the leading Jacobite families, tried to keep their options open by giving support simultaneously to the Prince and the government. They were more anxious to back a winner than a cause. In so far as there was a substantial cause — apart from the dynastic one — it was the promotion of French, as opposed to British interests. Recent research suggests that the French failure to exploit the rebellion fully was caused by the inefficiency of their bureaucracy, rather than by any lack of intention or will.

The state of the Highlands during the Forty-Five was as confused and traumatic as the situation in Ulster today, and there was a pretty even distribution of skulduggery and idealism between the two sides.

The barbarity of the victors after Culloden must be condemned, but we cannot overlook the fact that, if there had been no rebellion, there would have been no repression. And, if the victory had gone the other way, there is no reason to doubt that the repression would have been quite as severe. Only the victims would have been different.

It is a matter for legitimate pride that the ordinary people of the Highlands resisted the temptation to betray the fugitive Prince for gain, but against that we must set the activities of people on the other side like Robertson, who went to London at his own expense, and at his own risk, to plead for the lives of parishioners who had been "out", and some of whom had shown considerable hostility to himself.

According to tradition one of those whose life he saved had once threatened him with a sgian dubh, while another celebrated his release by carrying off, in triumph, the woman the minister had hoped to marry.

Although the *Ministear Laidir* was not a Lewisman, there were quite a number of Lewis ministers, or ministers of Lewis descent, who applauded Cumberland, in the same way, among them representatives of two of the leading island families, the Macaulays of Uig and the Morisons of Ness. When the descendants of Domhnull Cam, and the descendants of his mortal enemy, the Breitheamh, joined hands to support a Hanoverian against a Stuart dynasty, clearly there was a wind of change blowing in the islands.

The fact which is relevant to my Search for Lewis is that the activists of the Presbyterian cause were largely out of sympathy with the ordinary people of their time. Perhaps it would be more accurate to say they were "out of phase" with them. Eventually the ordinary people in most areas, came to accept their leaders' faith, (or ideology).

When we talk about the island way-of-life we must never forget that it is not static, but constantly evolving, and that almost everything we cherish has come to us originally from the world outside. Sometimes, in fact, has been imposed upon us.

That is not to say that the concept of an island way-of-life is an illusion. There is a relationship between the active minority (the instruments or harbingers of change), and the passive majority (the conservators of tradition) in any community, and especially in an island community, which is rather like the relationship between the conscious and the subconscious mind. As ideas pass from the area of conflict between opposing ideologies into the stage of settled and uncritical acceptance, a process of winnowing, assimilation and suppression takes place, in which the important matter is no longer the new, and controversial, acquisition, but the fusion of the new and the old. This produces a matrix — or mask — for the community, which gives it an apparent shape, but beneath this surface unresolved tensions still survive, occasionally disturbing the equilibrium.

This is an area of life which is difficult to explore, and where the jargon of sociology tends to obfuscate rather than reveal, but of which islanders, because of the intensity of their communal experience, have an instinctive, if inarticulate, grasp.

20
Hannah Ceard and Catriona Glas

The "silk and worsted waistcoat", stolen by the pirates from the master of the *Jane,* reminds me of a blue silk waistcoat, with a floral pattern in gold, which my grandfather had. I never saw it worn except once, when my brother borrowed it to appear with his cousin, Roddie Ross, as Darby and Joan, in a Boy Scout Fancy Dress Parade, incongruously riding a motor bicycle. The waistcoat was a gorgeous affair by the drab standard of male attire in Lewis in my youth. It suggested a much more colourful period in the past, when the dress of seafaring men was rich and romantic.

I find it difficult to associate the waistcoat with my grandfather because, as I remember him, he was a douce old man, sitting by the fire reading, or taking home the cow for his daughters to milk, and always soberly clad in black or navy. I was only seven when he died, and I was hardly aware that he had been a seaman. My grandmother and my uncle were the dominant influences in the family, and I was much more conscious of our connection with the church.

When my mother told me how, as a child, she made herself tipsy, in Liverpool, by drinking the dregs of port from the glasses on the hotel table, it never crossed my mind that my grandfather, and perhaps even my grandmother, might have had a glass of port themselves. I didn't even ask myself what my mother was doing in Liverpool, or visualise the journey she and my granny must have made in the conditions of that time. It must have been around 1880. Still less did I visualise the voyage my grandfather must have completed, in a sailing ship, returning from the far ends of the earth, when they went to meet him.

It was only recently I learned that my grandfather, in his last illness, created something of a minor scandal by asking for "a bottle of Bass's beer." His wish was gratified, but the procurement of a bottle of beer must have presented a problem in a strict teetotal household.

Once, as a child, when he was listening to some of my grandfather's stories, Willie Pope said to him in surprise, "You wouldn't drink a tot of rum, Uncle Rory!" "Indeed I would," was the reply. "And the other fellow's too, if I could lay my hands on it."

There is no one alive who can tell me how my grandfather adjusted to the austere life at home when he finally retired from the sea. He always seemed perfectly content, and the household was a happy one. Was he one of those fortunate individuals who can have his dram, or forgo it, with equal facility, or was it just accepted, and winked at, that he would slip off to town when he felt like it? It may well have been the latter, for the strict teetotalism in which I was nurtured crept up on the family (and the community) slowly.

The relationship of our family, and of Stornoway, to alcohol is an excellent illustration of the confused complexity of the process of ideological change, below the level of public controversy, to which I have referred. Different people move at different speeds, often in different directions. Only the historian, looking back from an eminence, can say with any certainty what the general drift of the current was at any particular moment. Those involved in the change are only conscious of their own position, relative to the flotsam round about them.

Once, when Bella and Jessie were confined to bed in their latter years, Anna came to them with a glass of sherry to drink a toast on some important family occasion. That surprised me because Anna was the staunchest teetotaler of all the sisters. What followed surprised me even more.

She gave the glass to Bella. Then she turned to Jessie and said, "You can't have one. You're a British Woman," — a reference to the fact that she and Jessie had been, many years before, members of the once-active British Women's Temperance Association. It was said with a smile, and seemed, on the surface, to be a joke. But it wasn't entirely. Jessie didn't get her sherry, then or later. Bella sipped away in splendid isolation.

I can only conclude that Bella, the oldest sister, was closer to her parents in her attitude to alcohol than either Anna or Jessie. They were younger, and had been more closely associated with my uncle's ministry, and his campaigning prohibitionism, because they had, for many years, kept house for him.

I don't think I ever heard it mentioned as a child that my great granduncle Colin had been a publican, although I was familiar with his name and with his portrait, which hung half way up the stair at Newton, and aroused my curiosity as one of the few oil paintings I had ever seen. Like many of the other objects in the house, it came from the Far East. A seafaring relative of Colin got it painted, from a photograph, in Hong Kong or Shanghai.

I was also familiar with Colin's magnificent set of the *Dictionary of National Biography,* in something like twenty leather bound volumes, which had passed to my grandfather on Colin's death. It suggests that Colin was a man of some culture, as well as a publican, a combination which would have troubled me greatly if I had been aware of it, because, at that time, alcohol, and anyone connected with it, were associated in my mind with the devil.

Colin came alive for me the other day when I read the story of his encounter with Hannah Ceard, who seems to have been a well-known character in the town in the closing years of last century. Hannah went to Colin's shop for a bottle of whisky. When it was safely in her basket, she announced that she had no money. But she would be in to pay for it, as sure as fate, the next time she was in town selling "tinnichan". Colin was adamant. He demanded the bottle back. Grumbling at his meanness, Hannah fumbled in her basket and handed the bottle across the counter. It was only after she had gone, Colin discovered it was another bottle, filled with water!

The story of how I stumbled on this little bit of gossip about my great granduncle, more than a hundred years after his death, and a similar incident involving another Stornoway worthy of the same vintage, Catriona Glas, leads on to a number of other things.

21
The Shop Assistants' Silver Stone

In 1854 a young man, named John Morison, left Stornoway for the Clyde. In a way he was a portent. His father was a master mariner, living on Keith Street: one of the captains who made the name of Stornoway respected in the great days of sail. I will come back to them later when I examine the involvement of Stornoway in the tea and opium trade. But that must wait for another volume.

John, however, was breaking new ground. He and Alexander Nicolson, founder of the Nicolson Institute, were the first Lewismen to become marine engineers, ushering in the age of the steamship. Their example was rapidly followed. When John Morison died, half a century later, it was estimated that there were around thirty Stornoway men holding first-class certificates from the Board of Trade. That must have represented one man out of every 25 in the working population of the town.

John Morison, as it happened, did not go to sea. He was disabled in an accident, and spent his working life in the shipyards of the Clyde. He was one of the stalwarts of the Lewis and Harris Association of Glasgow. Probably a founder member. He also kept in close touch with his native town, participating in the annual northward trek at the time of the Glasgow Fair: a mass pilgrimage of men, women and children which it is difficult to visualise today. On these visits north he delighted to recall the incidents of his youth. Especially the incidents he was involved in himself, when he worked, for a year or two, in Malcolm Macaulay's shop (or pub!), before he took up engineering.

The Stornoway shop assistants, and clerks, of that time were a special breed. For most of them, the stint behind the counter was just an interlude, a stepping stone to something better. That was how they earned the money to take them to university, or through an apprenticeship in Glasgow, or help them emigrate. Their eyes were always on a distant goal, rather than the immediate job, and the conditions under which they worked. They had a very active society, but it was not a trade union. Trade unions came later. It was more of the nature of a Literary and Debating Society. It was concerned with education, and self-improvement.

It would be interesting to know just how many men who made a reputation later as ministers, doctors, teachers, engineers, or men of business, in this country or abroad, earned the funds to get them started behind the counter in a Stornoway shop.

One of them even became a novelist. He was not very successful, or well known, but he did have a three-decker romance published by a London firm. It opens up a number of literary and social trails which are worth pursuing. One of them leads, rather unexpectedly, to the office of Donald Munro, who haunts these pages like a bad dream. There is a danger that this little bit of Scottish literary history may be lost sight of for good, unless I find an opportunity to explore it somewhere in these reminiscences.

So many Lewismen, at that time, took the shop assistants' route to fortune, a mythology grew up around them. There was a large stone, near where the Porter's Lodge stands today, which was known as Clach an Airgid—the Silver Stone, or the Money Stone. It was said that any boy, coming into Stornoway from a country village to start his career, who sat on that stone, would make his fortune. An interesting little superstition, evocative of the aspirations of Lewis lads when there was no easy access to the universities.

It was among the lads of this group, when he came back "home", year after year, John Morison would recall the stories of his own youth, and, in particular, the story of his encounter with Catriona Glas, who was reputed to keep a "speak-easy".

The word startled me when I came on it. I always thought we borrowed "speak-easy" from the Americans, and that they coined it during the era of Prohibition and Al Capone in the early twenties. *Collins Dictionary* takes the same view, while the *Shorter Oxford* does not mention "speak-easy" at all. My *Dictionary of Historical Slang* is equally silent. Yet there is irrefutable evidence that the word was in spoken, and written, use in Stornoway in 1911, and a strong inference that it was in common use in the town at a very much earlier date.

In any event, Catriona was in the habit of getting the supplies for her "speak-easy" from Malcolm Macaulay. One day when she placed her order, she asked John Morison, who served her, to put the bottles aside, and she would collect them on her way home. It seemed a reasonable request, and John complied. Catriona, however, timed her return to coincide with his lunch hour, and collected the bottles from his unsuspecting boss without telling him they had not been paid for.

Sometime later she tried the same approach. On this occasion John was ready for her. He would put nothing aside until he had the money in his hand. Reluctantly Catriona paid.

"Right!" said John. "That pays for the last order. Pay me now for this lot, and I'll put it aside for you." Catriona had met her match.

John told this story about himself, and the story about Hannah Ceard and Colin Morison, to Roddie Stephen, when he was a young man. Roddie Stephen recalled the stories in an obituary he wrote when John Morison died in 1911. By chance I came on an old newspaper cutting of the obituary the other day, and that was how I picked up a bit of gossip about my great granduncle, Colin Morison, more than a century after his death.

Clearly Colin, the publican, had a very different view of alcohol from his nephew, the minister and temperance reformer, who helped to make Stornoway dry, or nominally dry, around 1920. And the transition from the one stance to the other was made at different rates by different members of the family.

The attitude of the churches to alcohol seems to have moved in the same complex way. When I was a child I always believed, rightly or wrongly, that the Parish Church was much laxer, as I saw it, in its stance on drink than the United Free, to which I belonged, and which was deeply committed to the prohibition movement. Oddly enough, we regarded the Free Church and the Free Presbyterians as laxer still, on this particular issue. They were reputed to tolerate the use of whisky at weddings and funerals which, to us, was little short of mortal sin.

Today the Church of Scotland—even the old UF element in it—is much more tolerant of alcohol than it was in my youth, while the Free Church and the Free Presbyterians seem to have become the spearhead of prohibitionism.

It is almost as if, on social questions, as distinct from basic doctrinal issues, the various denominations are engaged in a slow and stately dance around each other. It is a situation which should engender humility, rather than dogmatism, in expressing points of view.

22
The Three Times of Tolsta

One can see the same differential time lag—to coin a phrase worthy of the sociologists—at work in regard to Sunday transport, as to temperance, so-called.

Many years ago I got a book from Canada entitled, "Can Sabbath-keeping Prevent Church-going?" It was a very detailed, and, in a legalistic sort of way, erudite, discussion on the question whether it was a greater sin to take a tram to church on Sunday, or to stay away altogether. The dilemma struck Lewis in the middle twenties with the arrival of the bus.

To begin with, all the churches were opposed to the use of motor transport even to go to church on Sunday, and all have come round to using it, to a greater or lesser degree. But their views changed at very different rates, and at each stage there were people, in each denomination, who assumed that their own views on the subject were correct, consistent and unchanged, and that all the others were either bigoted or damned.

There was one elder I knew of who insisted on walking to church long after buses were accepted by the rest of the congregation. One day the bus driver persuaded him to come in out of a rainstorm. He compromised by standing all the way to church. I have seen a minister driving to church through a downpour, passing his wife and family on the way, without giving them a lift. Presumably it was a work of necessity for him but not for them.

As a journalist I preferred to ignore these little inconsistencies rather than exploit them, although I might chuckle over them in private conversation. If I gave them any serious thought they made me wonder what my own particular foibles might be, for none of us are free from them. The question of Sabbath Observance became a public issue from time to time, however, notably during the long drawn out controversy over the Sunday sailing of the *Lochness*, the Stornoway mailboat.

The Town Council of Stornoway was ranged on one side of the argument, insisting that the steamer must leave in time to catch the early train from Kyle, even on Sunday night. A strong lobby on the other side, supported mainly by the Free Church and the Free Presbyterian Church, argued that the *Lochness* should not sail until after midnight on Sundays.

It became an issue at a Council election time, and one councillor at least, Malcolm Macdonald, one of the finest craftsmen I have ever known, came into public life, as it were, on a Sabbatarian ticket. He was an excellent councillor.

The argument against Sunday sailing seemed to me self-destructive because it asked too little. All that was argued for was that the departure should be after midnight. No account seemed to be taken of the work which must take place on board to prepare for departure. Equally no account seemed to be taken of the fact that a departure shortly after midnight would solve the problem for those who lived in Stornoway, but would not help a man, with strong Sabbatarian principles, who had to travel in from Uig. Appearances seemed to be more important than realities.

It was a lively controversy with much hard hitting on both sides. I find it difficult to recall the serious arguments, but I do remember some of the more humorous passages.

The then rector of the Nicolson Institute produced a little poem on the controversy, of which I can remember only the first verse:

The heathen in his blindness
Bowed down to wood and stone
But, knowing not chronometers,
He left the clock alone.

Somewhat similar issues were raised during the war when the Government introduced double summer time. It was said that in Tolsta the Church of Scotland adopted double summer time, the Free Church compromised on single summer time, and the Free Presbyterians stuck to Greenwich time.

The "Three Times of Tolsta" provoked my friend, Stephen MacLean, to write a letter drawing attention to the fact that Lewis is something like twenty-five minutes west of Greenwich, so the Sunday we observe is an artificial concept quite unrelated to the sun. He went on to show that the difference between sun time in Lewis, and sun time in Greenwich, changes slightly with the changing seasons, and explained the elaborate mathematical calculation that would have to be made by anyone who wanted to regulate himself precisely by the Lord's time, so called.

A few years later, when he was a qualified solicitor, Stephen was faced with the problem in a slightly different form. The bus drivers in Point came to seek his advice about a difficulty they had. They had inaugurated a Sunday service to Lewis hospital, which was quite a daring thing to do in the state of public opinion on Sunday travel at that time.

A great many people took advantage of the service, but refused, on principle, to pay on Sunday. They would pay on Monday! Unfortunately, when Monday came, many of them seemed to be suffering from amnesia. Stephen's advice was simple. "Except in dire emergencies, carry no one on Sunday who hasn't a ticket. And sell the tickets on Saturday." I had no personal experience of the matter, but I gathered that the advice was accepted, and worked.

The controversy over the Sunday sailing of the mail-steamer was eventually resolved when the *Loch Seaforth* replaced the *Lochness*. A speedier vessel, it was able to catch the early train at Kyle, without sailing until after midnight on any night.

On the first occasion on which Rev Kenneth Macrae, who had been a leader in the controversy, took advantage of the new arrangement, to permit him to get to Edinburgh for a church meeting on a Monday, he met Provost Mackenzie on the gangway, as he went on board. The conversation between the two leaders in a notable controversy was friendly, succinct, and pointed.

"Good evening, Mr Macrae!"   "Good morning, Provost!"

Although I disagreed with Mr Macrae vigorously over the Sunday sailing of the *Lochness* I had a very high regard for him. He was so unswervingly honest. On one occasion, at the height of the controversy, we met on Francis Street, on the way to church. We walked along together. He said to me with a smile, "A lot of people will be surprised to see us walking down the street together."

When we came to the County Hotel corner, he turned right for the Free Church. I turned left for Martin's. I think we both felt that the things that united us were a good deal more important than the things that divided us.

23
No Bicycles in the Bible

My uncle used to tell a story about a confrontation he had with an elder, when he was minister in Lochcarron, at the beginning of the century. He had cycled to church, because he had a long way to go, and there was no other way he could get there in time. The elder upbraided him for desecrating the Sabbath. What amused my uncle about the incident was that the elder had just stepped ashore from a boat, having rowed across the loch.

Presumably he went on the basis that there were boats in the Bible, but no bicycles.

A little later, my uncle was presented with a dilemma when he was asked to say grace over the whisky being dispensed at a funeral. As a strict teetotaler trying to suppress the service of drink at funerals, he had a rather delicate decision to make.

It was the same sort of dilemma which confronted a Lewis minister, nearly half a century later, when he criticised the Stornoway YMCA for running dances to raise funds for their wartime services canteen. I asked him if there was dancing at any of the weddings in his congregation. He replied that there might be, but it had nothing to do with the service, and nothing to do with him.

"But, if dancing is sinful, you should surely put a stop to it," I said to him. "You could refuse to marry folk, unless they gave an assurance there would be no dancing in the barn."

"If I did, I wouldn't have a congregation," he replied.

"Precisely!" I said.

He had the grace to smile, and I have no recollection that he repeated his attack on the YMCA.

When one gets bogged down in the legalistic minutiae of religion one almost inevitably ends up with an absurdity. It often worried me that we were prone to that sort of stupidity in Lewis, which represented the island in an unfavourable light to the outside world, and completely concealed the real core of the island's religious faith. What one might call the enduring substratum of belief, which extends beneath all the denominations (including that of our cousins in the southern isles, who are so very much like ourselves in all that matters), and which has persisted over the generations despite many social and ecclesiastical upheavals.

In the reporting of church affairs it is unfortunately true that it is, normally, the superficial, the irrelevant, which makes headlines. It was always difficult to know what to do when something of that sort occurred, like the criticism of the YMCA for their method of fund-raising, or the spicy words of reproof used by a minister, on a public bus, to a girl wearing jeans!

On the one hand there was the reformers' zeal to knock at folly—and earn an honest penny, or a few extra sales, in the process. On the other there was the Lewisman's desire to hide his shame, and spare his fellow islanders' blushes.

When I was the only reporter in Stornoway, I sometimes exercised my discretion and imposed a little private censorship on the news. Once one is in a competitive situation, however, the game becomes entirely different. In journalism bad news tends to drive out good: the trivial, the serious.

A more difficult problem in knowing what to report, and how to report it, was raised by an unusual religious revival which swept through Lewis, just before the Second World War. We were used to passionate, hearty, psalm-singing revivals (hymn-singing if they affected the English rather than the Gaelic community). Dramatic individual conversions were also common. But this was something quite out of the ordinary.

It began, if I remember rightly, in a house in Parc, but it spread to Point. which seemed to become the focal centre of the movement. It was distinguished from the normal revival by the violent physical convulsions which sometimes occurred at the meetings. Some participants went into trances. Some held their arms upraised rigidly, for hours, without apparent fatigue. Some bounced violently up and down, in their seats, in a way they could not voluntarily do. The singing of certain psalms, I was told by Rev Kenneth Macrae, seemed to produce more violent physical reactions than others.

The island was not affected generally. The movement was confined to pockets here and there. Many of those who were involved were comparatively young. In fact I think I would be correct in saying that it was a movement of the young, rather than the elderly, although all age groups were affected to some degree.

But the young folk who stood aside from it—the great majority—poured scorn on those who were drawn in. They referred to the movement rather disparagingly as the "cliobadaich". The inadequacies of the English language being made good, as so often, in descriptions of personal appearance or behaviour, by the use of a much more pictorially apt word from the older tongue.

It was not only from the secular side there was criticism of the movement. There was a sharp difference of opinion even within the churches, and the division ran along a rather unexpected line. It was not denominational. It did not separate right and left, if one might use these terms in a non-political area. Ministers who might be termed moderate, liberal, enlightened, or unsound—according to the standpoint from which one viewed them—tended to go along with the revival, in spite of the disturbing physical manifestations. The criticism came from the other end of the spectrum. Notably from the Rev Kenneth Macrae.

And from some of the island doctors, although so far as I recall, none of them made any public pronouncement. One doctor said to me, "If a man has appendicitis they call a doctor, but, when a man is tortured in his mind, they throw a party, call it a service, and all the neighbours come to gloat!"

It was without doubt one of the most difficult patches of shoal water I ever had to sail through as a reporter. I decided that, in so far as it was reported at all, the only stance I could take was to try to present the views of all the different factions in the most favourable way possible, as they would see it themselves.

Which was not very easy, unless one had been intellectually neutred.

24
Neil Gunn and the Silver Darlings

When the revival was at its height, Neil Gunn, then making a name for himself as a novelist, came to Lewis to stay with his friend Dr P. J. Macleod. Neil was writing *The Silver Darlings* and the primary purpose of his visit was to go to the Flannan Isles, with Calum Sheorais from Bernera, PJ's father, to get material for the great cliff-climbing scene in the book, which must rank as one of the finest Scottish novels written this century.

Neil was very interested when he heard of the revival, and I can recall an amusing evening in PJ's when it was being planned that John Macsween, then headmaster at Aird, would take Neil to one of the house meetings in Point. It was clear that John was having an intense internal struggle between his wish to accommodate a distinguished visitor, and good friend, as a hospitable Lewisman should, and his determination not to get involved as a "snooper".

Incidentally, it was another leading Scottish novelist I once heard singing John Macsween's praises as an orator of great distinction. Eric Linklater and John had been fellow students at Aberdeen, and Linklater gave me a graphic description of a dinner he had attended. I think it was a dinner of the Aberdeen Celtic Society. "John was standing on the table when he spoke", said Linklater. "In fact he was marching up and down between the glasses. He spoke in Gaelic. I didn't understand a single word he said, but I have no doubt that it was the most eloquent speech I have ever heard."

John Macsween's claim on our gratitude does not, however, rest on his Gaelic oratory, but on the solid work he did at Aird, especially in his navigation class, and his later achievement as the first Principal of Lews Castle Technical College, which has produced a new race of Gaelic Vikings.

Although I was amused by John's reluctance to take Neil Gunn to a revivalist meeting, and his equal reluctance to refuse outrightly, I could understand his position. In fact I shared it. Although I was a journalist, I had a disabling respect for other people's privacy which often made me seek my information at second hand. One step back from the event. I am not at all sure that I did not get to know the community more completely, and accurately, in that way, than if I had thrust myself into the island's viscera, scalpel, (and notebook) in hand.

No doubt I could have got a good colour piece, if I had gone to one of the meetings. But what would the effect of my presence have been on the meeting itself? Would the presence of a stranger, with a notebook, have put a damper on the proceedings? Or would those involved have played to the gallery? I have no doubt it would have had both effects simultaneously. The more timid, and perhaps the more sincere, might well have been restrained by the prospect of publicity. The exhibitionists would have "gone to town".

The intrusion of a reporter into a situation of that sort changes the situation significantly. This is especially true of television cameras. What is eventually recorded is not what would have happened in the reporter's absence, which is the real truth of the event, but what happened in the reporter's presence, which is another matter altogether.

If I had been a complete insider, it might have been different. I could have gone to the meetings without question. But then my reporting would have been different too. And much less objective.

Just as, in my ignorance of Gaelic, I was one of a small intrusive minority, despite the fact that my mother's family had lived in Lewis for centuries, so in my views on religion, politics, and almost everything else, I was somewhat out of step, or out of phase, with the majority of my fellow islanders. I claimed, and exercised, the right to express my own views without inhibition in the leader column of the paper, but, in the news, and especially in the correspondence columns, I felt it was my duty to present the views of other people as accurately as I could, and in the most favourable possible light, however much I disagreed with them. It was a severe discipline, and I cannot pretend that I lived up to the standard I set myself. But I did succeed to the extent that I was able to speak, on easy terms, with the representatives of all shades of island opinion, however remote from my own.

Although I was not prepared to conform, I could never persuade myself that I was necessarily right, and the rest of mankind wrong. I was never a rebel. Perhaps I lacked the spirit to rebel. Perhaps I was influenced by the fact that my bread and butter, as owner of the local newspaper, depended on striking some sort of compromise between the majority views and my own. But I was not prepared to dodge delicate issues and comment on nothing. I was sufficient of an egoist to think it was my duty to convert the island to my own ideas, but sufficient of a realist to know that I had to do it without pressing my views so far as to create an open rupture.

In that situation it was not possible for me to attend the revivalist meetings. I could have gone only as a participant—or a spy. A complete outsider, like Neil Gunn, might perhaps have gone as a detached observer, although even that would have changed the nature of the meeting, but, if you are part of a community, you cannot attend a sectarian occasion, especially when it is of a private nature, without taking sides.

The result is that my knowledge of Lewis is mainly derivative, and slightly out of focus, even although I spent the greater part of my life in the island. But I flatter myself that I have a more balanced, and perhaps a more complete view, than many who know parts of the island's life more intimately, but see it all from a very personal point of view, or through the distorting mirror of a deeply held ideology.

My information about the revival came mainly from participants, especially some of the ministers, and they presented me with two sharply contrasting views.

82

25
The Crazy Machismo of the Pubs

The Rev Kenneth Macrae was very critical of the emotionalism, and the physical manifestations, associated with the pre-war revival. It was a difficult situation for him because he was an evangelical preacher himself. There was nothing he wanted more than to see a great religious revival in Lewis. But he wanted a revival of substance, in his terms, not froth.

He expressed his misgivings freely in public, while in his diary he refers dismissively to the "jerks". He wanted nothing to do with exhibitionism. It required great courage to take such a line in the mood prevailing, but he was never afraid to stand alone. He was criticised within his own church, and even within his own congregation, for his views. As far as I could gather, the most heinous aspect of his offence, in the eyes of his critics, was that he quoted from medical text-books on a religious subject. They saw that, not only as heresy, but almost as blasphemy.

Mr Macrae's misgivings about the revival were not based primarily on medical evidence, however. They were based on the experience of earlier revivalists who were embarrassed by occurrences on the periphery of their own campaigns which, in their view, had nothing to do with religion.

The Rev Harry Mackinnon, the Church of Scotland Minister at Garrabost, who was right at the heart of the revival, also had misgivings about some of the manifestations, but he believed, as he told me, that they were "one phase of the working of the Holy Spirit." A gentle, sensitive soul, Harry Mackinnon saw good in everything. He lacked the dry toughness of Kenneth Macrae.

He was quite clearly troubled when he described for me a prayer meeting in a private house at which people fell into trances, or became rigid for long periods in a quite unnatural way. One girl, he told me, cried out that there was someone present who did not accept Christ. The meeting then became uproarious. Seven or eight people were on their feet shouting, "Who is it? Who is it?" A young lad in another room broke down, weeping violently, and those, who had been shouting, stood up rejoicing that he had been saved. They shook him by the hand, congratulating him, while he cried out repeatedly, like a refrain, "Na balaich eile, c'ait a bheil iad?"*

The fact that the cry has a very marked rhythm in Gaelic is not, I think, without significance. Slogans and catchwords can be very potent, as every advertiser knows.

Harry Mackinnon told me that the regular church meetings were not so

*"The other boys, where are they?"

boisterous as the prayer meetings in private houses, and many of the older church-goers did not approve of the physical manifestations and shouting, at all. When an elder prayed at one service that they might have a peaceful meeting, some of the younger men reproved him, asking whether it was better to have a peaceful meeting, or one at which souls were saved.

He did not feel himself in any danger of being carried away by the emotionalism, he told me. But, at one of the early meetings, when members of the congregation were affected by violent shaking, he felt as if there was an electric shock passing through him. It seemed to come from the table on which he was leaning, but, even when he lifted his elbows off the table, the sensation continued. Those who were first affected, he believed, were genuinely carried away by religious enthusiasm, but those who joined in the demonstrations latterly could have controlled themselves, if they had tried. That seems to accord with Kenneth Macrae's view that there was a considerable element of exhibitionism.

Men and women were both affected, Harry Mackinnon told me, but women more frequently than men. They ranged in age from their teens to over sixty. Even at the height of the revival the numbers affected were comparatively small. He reckoned twenty or thirty in his own congregation, and perhaps a similar percentage in the larger Free Church congregation.

One side effect of the revival was that, in a village where the two denominations had been antagonistic, they came together to hold joint services. But that, I am afraid, was a passing phenomenon.

The reaction of Kenneth Macrae's critics to his use of medical text-books recalls an occasion in my boyhood when there was a head-on collision between medical opinion in the island, and the churches.

There was an incipient epidemic, possibly scarlet fever, but I cannot be sure. Epidemics were much more frequent then, and much more alarming, than they are today. There was very little provision locally for coping with them. The isolation hospital was a tiny little building at Mossend, serviced by a rickety ambulance, which was known, expressively, as the "fever van". The half yearly communion season was just about to begin. The MOH was worried at the possibility of the epidemic spreading rapidly and out of control through the whole island. The old custom of going to neighbours at communion time for a three or four day visitation was still in full vigour. To it had just been added, for the first time, the mobility, and novelty, of the motor bus. The whole population of the island was about to be stirred around like a vast porridge pot. The MOH suggested that in the interests of health, and indeed of life, the communion services should be postponed. The ministers were aghast. They regarded the suggestion as both irreligious and impertinent.

My recollection is rather hazy. I was just a kid at the time. More interested in football than in communions or epidemics, but my recollection is that the services went ahead as planned, while the epidemic ran its course without being unduly disastrous. No doubt both parties to the argument felt able to claim that the outcome vindicated their judgment.

84

It required the same sort of courage from the MOH, at that time, to suggest the postponement of the communion services, as it required of Kenneth Macrae to speak out against the hysteria associated with the later revival. It always takes courage to swim against the tide.

There is danger in any situation in which a long-established tradition, or a massive majority opinion, weighs heavily on the non-conformist—even if the majority is right and the non-conformist wrong. It encourages intellectual sloth, and hypocrisy. Breeds self-complacency and arrogance.

Of course, it is not only from religion that heavy pressure to conform can come. There is no greater tyranny affecting the lives of young islanders today than the social pressures towards heavy drinking.

We cannot solve the problem by exchanging the tyranny of prohibition for the tyranny of conformity to social codes. Prohibition is not a rallying cry likely to stir the young to action. In any event it is a misinterpretation of the problem. It is not in the name of prohibition, but in the name of personal freedom, we should seek to break the social codes which now enslave us. The almost inescapable obligation to match round with round. The absurd pride which makes us try to show that we can hold our drink, which, ironically, is at its strongest when we manifestly cannot. The self-assertiveness which makes us resent the reasonable refusal of our proferred hospitality.

In short—the whole crazy machismo of the pubs.

The tyranny of those who call themselves our friends.

26
The Thunder is in Good Hands

Those who stood aside from the revival made fun of it. It became very difficult to know which of the stories in circulation had a basis in fact, and which were invented by the scoffers. When it was reported that a woman on the West Side claimed to have seen Christ, that might well have been true. In the mood prevailing, hallucinations would not have been surprising. When the story went round that the spring work had come to a standstill, in one of the villages, because the end of the world was expected on Friday, it was the Lewis sense of humour asserting itself.

It was said that on one occasion the congregation in a Mission house in Parc heard a tremendous shower of hail rattling on the roof until the whole place dirled. When they got outside, they discovered that it had been a fine evening without even a drop of rain.

I asked someone I could rely on in the district about the story. He told me he had not heard it. But he had heard of a house which was shaken as if by a tremendous wind during a service. The illusion, he said, did not surprise him, because there must have been two hundred people crowded into it at the time. It was such a flimsy structure it might have collapsed altogether under the pressure.

He added that, according to his information, the revival had begun in the home of an elderly lady who, up until then, had no particular interest in religion, but who suddenly claimed that she had received a heavenly message that she was not to move out of her attic until the village was converted. People then began to flock to her. She was regarded as a special messenger.

My informant said he was under pressure from many of his neighbours to go to her and seek a blessing. He didn't go. He did, however, attend some of the more general meetings. At two of them, about a dozen people were affected with shouting and trembling. At the third nothing happened out of the ordinary, and the missionary drew the conclusion that the spirit of God had not been with them.

The revival died out very quickly after the outbreak of war. Some of the leaders did continue to hold meetings for some months but the fire was spent. So far as I know, the only permanent effect one can trace is some fine writing in Neil Gunn's *The Silver Darlings*, describing an imaginary revival in a Lewis village, half a century before.

The pre-war revival was given its shape by the ecclesiastical traditions of the island, and the long history of involvement by eloquent lay preachers in the services. But where did the element of hysteria come from, which is so foreign to us, and which caused so much concern to Rev Kenneth Macrae, and some of the local doctors?

One can only speculate, but I am sure the impetus came, in part at least, from the distressed social and economic conditions in the island in the twenties and thirties. As I have already pointed out, Lewis had a grossly unbalanced population, as a result of the mass emigration after the First World War, coming on the heels of exceptionally heavy war losses, and the *Iolaire* disaster.

In addition, the economy of the island was in disarray. The herring fishing industry was in decline, both locally and nationally. Hundreds of men and women who had relied on it for a living were out of work, and without unemployment benefit.

It was the era of the Means Test. Of relief work on the roads to which, ironically, the workers themselves had to make a contribution in the form of "free" labour, calculated in such a way that, at times, the earnings of a labourer fell to two pence halfpenny per hour.

Although the tweed industry was expanding, thanks to the amendment of the Orb Trade Mark, it did not take up the slack, and the employment provided was not necessarily in the villages most severely affected by the decline in the fishing.

It was a period of economic and social distress throughout the whole of Western Europe. In the urban areas of Britain the pressures found some outlet in political activity, like the hunger marches, but left behind a legacy of bitterness which influences our judgment on public affairs even to the present day. In Germany, where conditions were even worse, the distresses of the twenties and thirties produced Hitler, who fostered and canalised the despair, with the skill not of a dictator but a demagogue. A distinction we should never forget.

The question is not why there was tension and hysteria in Lewis at that time, but why there was so little. The general stability of the social structure under extreme pressure was quite astonishing. It suggests that the foundations of family and religious life were sound, and that the croft, which kept people active even when they were out of a job, protected them from the hopelessness which affected the cities.

The demonstrative revivalism I have been writing of is not characteristic of Lewis, nor indeed is the rabid, divisive, sectarianism which is peddled by those who have positions of power to protect, and which sometimes hits the headlines.

In a classless community with few outlets for intellectual ability or leadership—as Lewis was during the period of which I write—the church was inevitably used—or misused—by the ambitious to establish their own position in the pecking order. It is a danger which it is difficult to guard against, in any structure which gives even the illusion of personal power. One of the last and subtlest of temptations.

The intellectual jousting of activists, using theology as the earthworks round little personal kingdoms, has nothing to do with the deep, underlying spirituality on which the life of Lewis rests. Whenever I was distressed by the publicity attracted by some petty "bull" emanating from synod or presbytery, I thought of the serene faith of my grandmother, sitting blind, but erect, in bed, as she talked to me when I sat beside her, a little impatiently, I must confess, for a few moments every Sunday afternoon. Or the comment of the old lady from Laxdale who said to me during the war, "When I heard the 'tuirlich', I thought it was an air raid. But, as soon as I knew it was thunder, I was quite content. The thunder is in good hands."

Or of Angus Murray from South Shawbost, who saved the lives of seventeen shipmates, when their ship was torpedoed in mid-Atlantic, guiding them through heavy seas for nine and a half days, with a sail improvised from blankets and an oar. Nothing was heard of his achievement in Lewis, even after he came home, until the wife of one of his English shipmates enquired for his address so that she could thank him.

When I tried to prise from him some details of a voyage, which began with an upturned boat from which radio, mast, oars, sail, and provisions had all been lost, he said, simply, "I know a little about boats right enough, and that's all very well, but I am thankful to God that I came out of it alive, because that's what I believe, and I trust in it."

27
The Tolsta Chaolais Poltergeist

On an earlier visit to Lewis, Neil Gunn had been very interested in another island phenomenon—the Tolsta Chaolais poltergeist. He arrived at P.J.'s on the day I was investigating the mystery, and he was quite disappointed, when I called in the evening with what to me, and quite a lot of other people, seemed a rational explanation of what occurred.

On a Monday morning, when I was making my usual trawl for news through the town, I heard that strange things had been happening the previous day, in a house in Tolsta Chaolais. Quite apart from the whiff of news, I was glad of the excuse to pay the area a visit. "Tolsta Chaolais with its back to the sea" is one of the most attractive of the Lewis villages, although many visitors to the West Side miss it altogether.

I asked Dan MacGregor, the librarian, to come with me. As a native of the village I thought people might speak more freely to him than to me, about something that might be troubling them. Dan readily agreed. He was curious to find out what had really happened in his native village. Also perhaps he felt he owed it to me.

Very shortly before that I had spilt a bottle of ink on the office desk. Before I could take avoiding action, it had run over the edge on to my natty new grey flannel trousers. I had to get them dyed, and the only colour that would hide the stain was bottle green. No one would turn a hair today if I walked down the street in bottle green flannels. In this informal, permissive age I might even get by without trousers at all—apart from the draught. It was very different in the mid thirties. Business men at that time dressed very formally, and when I ventured into the library for the first time, in my exotic trousers, Dan buried his face in a shelf of books and groaned like a Jew at the Wailing Wall. Then he challenged me to walk down Cromwell Street with him. In a moment of weakness I agreed. All the way along the street, he kept up a running commentary on my appearance, in a loud voice and louder language. When the colour of my trousers failed to startle people, Dan's picturesque speech made amends. I never felt so conspicuous in my life.

Donald, of course, could take the Mickey out of himself as well as out of other people. He loved to tell the story of the game of golf he played with a visiting minister, whom he did not really know. Donald duffed his drive off the first tee. Remembering the company he was in, he gritted his teeth and said nothing. The visitor, sizing the situation up, said quietly, "That was the most profane silence I ever listened to."

One evening on the golf course, Donald and I were held up by a player who took an inordinate time over every putt. I fumed and fretted and went off my game. Donald acted. He walked over to the offender, when he was bent over his club, nose down, contemplating his putt for what seemed an eternity. Tapping him on the shoulder, Donald asked, "In your last incarnation, were you a pointer?"

With Donald's aid I had no difficulty in establishing what had happened in Tolsta Chaolais. The eye witnesses spoke to us freely, and I have no doubt whatever that they told us the truth.

On Sunday morning an old lady, who lived in a little timber house, perched on a spur of rock, on a corner of the family croft, was having a cup of tea. Two of her grandchildren, a boy and a girl, were spending the week-end with her. As she sat in the bedroom, which also served as living room, sipping her tea, the caorans* began to jump from beside the very large cast-iron cooking stove, which stood in a corner of the room. One caoran hit her on the cheek. Another plopped into her cup of tea. Then there was a crash, and half the glass chimney of the hanging lamp lay in fragments on the floor.

The old lady was startled, but did not lose her head. She told her grand-daughter to take the dishes through to the little scullery which opened off the main room. As soon as the connecting door was opened, pandemonium broke loose. A jug of peasemeal, which had been standing on the scullery sink, came sailing into the bedroom and landed on the bed. A jug of rice followed, but fell in fragments on the floor. The teapot came sailing round the corner of the door, and struck the wall, high above the bed, spattering tea and tea leaves on the wallpaper.

While this was happening, the girl was holding the breakfast dishes against her chest for safety. The boy, who was just a toddler, sat on the floor, clapping his hands, and shouting excitedly in Gaelic, "Here's another! Here's another!" It was the best fun he ever had in his life.

Deciding that it was unsafe to put the dishes down on the sink, the grand-daughter hurried across to the cupboard, which was in the scullery beside the back door. As soon as she opened the cupboard door, most of the dishes there broke in pieces where they stood.

At this stage, the old lady's son, and other members of the family, on their way to church, heard the noise of breaking dishes, and hurried in to see what on earth was wrong.

It was then discovered that a row of cups, which had been hanging by their lugs from nails near the sink, had all been broken. The cups had fallen to the floor, but the lugs were dangling from the nails. The plates on the sink were also cracked clean across. The old lady's toothbrush was broken in two. The cake of Lifebuoy soap was cut into three pieces, as cleanly as if someone had done it with a knife. The only dishes left whole in the house were those the grand-daughter was still clinging to.

The incident gave rise to all sorts of stories in the village. There were many who were afraid to pass the house after dark. The old lady herself, however,

*small peats

had a clear mind and remarkable strength of character. She continued to live there, alone. When one of the elders called to warn her that the incident had been a judgment from on high, because she was houseproud, and made an idol of her dishes, she looked him straight in the eye and said, "You better be careful. You worship your cow!"

When I questioned her, the day after it happened, she was completely rational about it. "I don't understand it," she said, "but I know there is an explanation."

I think I know what it might be.

28
The Plane Made its Own Fog

At first glance, the Tolsta Chaolais incident has all the marks of the classical poltergeist, the racketing, or unruly, spirit with the German name, which has engaged the attention of Psychical Researchers for the past hundred years or more.

The term poltergeist is used to describe frequently recurring cases of strange noises being heard, which cannot be accounted for in any rational way, movements of furniture for no apparent reason, and breakages of crockery, which appear to be inexplicable to the residents in the house where they have occurred. Many well-documented cases, in all these categories, have been recorded over the centuries, and from all parts of the world, both civilised and barbarous.

Frequently there is a teenage girl involved, as the active agent of the disturbance, but there is seldom any logical motive to account for her strange behaviour. Occasionally there is fairly obvious trickery. Sometimes the trickery is so subtle that only a trained observer can detect it. Sometimes there is no evidence of trickery at all. Where trickery has been found, it often seems to be almost subconscious on the part of the trickster. Poltergeist has been described as a hysterical fraud, an attempt to draw attention to oneself, by a person who is not really conscious of what she is doing, or of her motive for doing it.

In Tolsta Chaolais we had the broken crockery. Plenty of it! We also had the presence of a teenage girl. And we had the mystery of why and how it all occurred. As a friend said to me at the time, "I know the old lady well. She's certainly not the sort of person who would break all the dishes in the house, just to make the neighbours talk."

The Society for Psychical Research showed interest in the case as soon as it occurred, but quickly dropped it. I suspect that, like myself, they had come to the conclusion that there was a natural, if unusual, explanation and that no poltergeist was involved.

Normally, in cases of poltergeist, the incidents occur over a period of time. So far as I know, the Tolsta Chaolais incident was "one off", as they say. It all happened on a Sunday morning without prior warning or recurrence. Moreover the old lady, who seemed a very clear-headed and accurate witness, was satisfied that her grand-daughter was carrying the breakfast dishes in her arms throughout the whole incident. She hadn't a free hand with which to throw things, even if she had wanted to. The breaking of the cups from their lugs, the chopping up of the toothbrush, the breaking of the hanging lamp globe, and the throwing of the caorans would not have been done very easily without being seen.

My belief is that the incident occurred precisely as the witnesses described it to me, and that it was due to an electrical disturbance.

It occurred around the time of day when electrical disturbances are at their maximum. It also occurred during a period of quite unusual electrical activity all over Europe. It was a weekend characterised by brilliant displays of aurora borealis at night, and violent thunderstorms by day.

Ian Maclean and I, who shared a dilletante interest in astronomy, had spent hours, the night before the incident, watching the aurora from the open road near Airidh na Lic. It wasn't the familiar curtain of green, shimmering across the sky. There were great gouts of pink and crimson light dancing all around us, from the horizon right to the zenith, and, at times, well into the southern sky. We were reminded of the tremendous closing speech in Marlowe's Faustus—"See! See! Where Christ's blood streams in the firmament."

Another feature which points to an electrical disturbance was the construction of the house. If there was any unusual electrical disturbance around, the house was a perfect Leyden jar, in which the charge would be built up, as I used to see it done, in the school laboratory. The wooden house provided the non-conducting container. Inside it was a disproportionately large iron stove, with an iron chimney projecting through the roof. The first indication that something unusual was happening came when the caorans began to jump away from the stove, as the room became charged with electricity via the chimney. Many of the later movements were caused as objects in the rest of the house began to move towards the highly charged room, once the non-conducting doors were opened.

A few months after the incident the old lady had occasion to darn a sock. She used a ball of wool, which she had found, on the day of the poltergeist (which was not a poltergeist), lying on the floor where it should not have been. She assumed it had been accidentally swept by someone passing, from the place where it was normally kept, and thought no more about it. But when she tried to darn a sock with it, the wool crumbled in her hand.

The significance of that was pointed by an incident in West Uig not long afterwards. A crofter, out working on his fence, was struck by lightning and thrown to the ground. He was uninjured, but his trousers were ripped off. Some time later it was discovered that all the clothes kept in a trunk in the house had mysteriously perished, just like the ball of wool.

Lewis gets comparatively little lightning, but over the years I have recorded quite a few freakish incidents, although none of them were quite as freakish as the tropical storm of which my grandfather used to speak. According to him, a flash of lightning ran along one of the ship's chains, cutting the links in two. But it welded them together again, as they fell, with the result that, after the flash, the chain had twice as many links as before!

That may just be a seaman's tale, but the weather does play strange pranks at times, like the fog which enveloped Stornoway airport some years ago, and aroused great interest in the scientific press.

It was a cold, clear, sunny winter day, with several inches of snow on the runway. The visibility couldn't have been better. The snow was actually "steaming" in the sunshine, when a BEA Pionair began to taxi. The draught from the propellors threw small particles of snow in a swirling cloud to a height of 40 or 50 feet. In a few minutes, a very clean, dense, white fog spread across the whole airport. The controller, in his tower, could see over it to the blue sky overhead. The plane was lost in the fog below. Unable to move.

The startled meteorologist saw the temperature in his Stevenson screen drop abruptly to 13.9 deg F. Nearly 20 deg below freezing point! Only marginally above the lowest temperature ever recorded in Lewis. But, at rooftop level, the snow was still melting briskly in the sun.

A short time later, a light breeze dispersed the fog.

29
The Song of the Bernera Bachelors

Years after the Tolsta Chaolais incident, I had a letter from the boy who sat on the floor, clapping his hands in glee, as the plates whizzed by. By this time he was a young man, on National Service, and he wrote about a well in the village, which, he alleged, was much resorted to by childless women, because it had aphrodisiac qualities.

The story, I suspect, was a leg-pull although it might have had a basis in local folklore. The well was certainly unusual in that it never ran dry, even in the hottest summer. When water was short elsewhere—as it very often was in early summer in those days—this particular well was in great demand, much to the annoyance of the old lady on whose croft it was. She acknowledged the right of only one neighbour to draw water from it. Each summer, over quite a period of years, I received transcripts of the latest notice posted on the well by the old lady. Generally they were written on a postcard, nailed to a stick. The best of them, that I remember, read, "Anyone found transpasing on this wel except Mrs Macleod and her denpendens is libel to prostitution."

If the serviceman's story about the properties of the well were, by any chance, true the punishment for "transpasing" might not have been quite so improbable as it sounded.

The addiction of a small minority to religious controversy has not only given outsiders a false impression of the true character of the church community, it has created the myth that we are a gloomy people. Far from it! Lewis is bubbling over with fun and mischief. The letter from the Tolsta Chaolais serviceman was just one example.

On one occasion I got a death notice with rather peculiar wording. The girl who took it, at the counter, came to me for advice. "There's something wrong with this notice", she said. "I don't think we should print it."

The notice read, "Deaths. Macleod. At the home of Mrs Macleod, (address given), Daisy, aged 23 years. Deeply mourned and sadly missed."

I read the advertisement and, in my superior wisdom, I saw at a glance that Daisy was an illegitimate daughter. The notice had obviously been drafted with great care to skirt round the fact. It was only after it appeared I discovered that Daisy was a cow. A celebrated cow. The whole village had watched with awe as the old lady had milked it to the very last drop. The "boys" thought its passing should not go unmarked.

It was good for my ego to have the West Side laughing at me. It was even better to be taken down a peg in the eyes of my own staff. Thereafter I paid more attention to their views.

On another occasion I got an advertisement from Bernera which puzzled me. A matrimonial advertisement, with rather peculiar wording. I suspected that it had been sent in by the youths of the village, and that the name on the covering letter was that of some crusty old bachelor, who had no idea what was going on. I decided to check it out, and wrote to the given name and address, asking whether it was genuine, and counselling against publication. Back came a letter assuring me that the advertisement was genuine, and asking for insertion, at an early date. I still hesitated, because I did not like it. But I felt I had committed myself by asking for instructions, and finally put it in.

The advertisement was perfectly genuine, in that it came from the person whose signature it bore. But he had no intention of marrying. He was a sailor, who had come back to his native village, and found it too dull for his liking. The population of the village was composed, almost entirely, of bachelors and spinsters. He thought he should do something about it. He framed the advertisement, cunningly, to identify the village while concealing the advertiser.

All hell was let loose. The women were insulted. The men were scared.

The first indication I had that things were livening up was an urgent message from the advertiser, asking me not to send any replies to him. I don't think he expected any genuine replies. He was probably afraid that some other jokers would send in bogus answers—as in fact they did—and that the arrival of a batch of mail at his address would "put the finger on him".

He said that, if any replies did come in, I was to hand them to a young friend of his, who was working in Stornoway. The young man, as it happened, was also a friend of mine. His sister had been in my class at school. From that point on I had the inside story. A ringside seat, so to speak.

One of the leading figures in the village tried to worm the identity of the advertiser out of me. He guessed the advert was a fake, suspected, for some reason, that his own name might have been used, and was scared, like the advertiser himself, that a sudden increase in the volume of his mail might have all the spinsters in the countryside beating at his door—or his person.

When I refused to disclose the advertiser's name, the inquirer drew up a solemn document to be signed by every man in the village, declaring, on oath, that he (the signatory) had not inserted the advertisement. In this way he hoped to flush out the culprit. The man who wouldn't sign was the one to hang!

The old sailor, at this stage, came back to me with his dilemma. It was all a leg-pull. What should he do? Refuse to sign and be crucified? Or tell a lie?

I'm afraid I took the easy way out. I told him, "You dug the hole, brother!"

Then events took a turn which is typical of Lewis, and illustrates what a real community is all about. When the bodachs realised it was a joke, at their expense, they joined in the fun themselves. So did Bernera people living away from home. One of them sent me, from Glasgow, a poem entitled, *The Reply of the Bernera Bachelors*, to the tune of that mournful ditty, *Oh, Jimmy, take your hankie out.*

The "poet" mentioned each of the bachelors by name, and advanced the most improbable reasons for their reluctance to enter the blessed state of matrimony. The staidest citizen of all was alleged to have replied: "To keep the peace, I favour none—that is, in public view—but on the quiet I'm Don Juan, a-courting quite a few!"

The poem was dynamite—and libel. I told the author so. His reply may surprise those who do not know the island. He said he would circularise the victims, and get their consent to publication.

A few weeks later I had a telegram from him: "Consent to publication immediately granted on request. The 'boys' are all good sports, and the best of fellows."

That, for me, is Lewis.

30
Mens Sana in Corpore Sano

The poem about the Bernera Bachelors was not an isolated incident. I will have occasion later to refer to the Breve and his Brevities, which performed an important social function for Lewis—a therapeutic function—at a difficult time of transition.

Before the Breve, and in the same tradition, there was Alasdair Mor's *Bernera Letter*.

The writer, John N. Macleod, was one of the leading Gaelic scholars of his generation, and he contributed a weekly letter to the *Gazette* for many years, beginning, if I remember rightly, with the very first edition. At that time he was teaching in Bernera, and wrote about the island directly, but he continued the letters when he became headmaster at Kirkhill, near Beauly. His wife was from Bernera, and, even after he left the island, Alasdair Mor was in close contact with the day to day happenings there.

The letters dealt with real people, and often with real events, but he let his fancy play so that the inhabitants of Bernera became characters in a world of fiction, slightly larger than life. He didn't mock anyone, for mockery is mean and ungracious, but he gently highlighted known characteristics, and idiosyncracies, for the delectation of all—including the victims.

The Bernera Letter was a valuable contribution to Gaelic literature, because it helped to maintain a rich vocabulary in popular use, at a time when the language was being impoverished by quite unnecessary borrowings from English. But it was even more important as a social document illustrating how a close-knit community really functions.

The acceptance of one's own idiosyncracies, even weaknesses, as part of the natural order of things is typical of Lewis—of the whole of the Hebrides for that matter.

Islanders only lose this sturdy realism, this sense of their own place in an integrated social fabric, if they leave home, and begin to rise in the world, and not always wholly then. Or perhaps if they begin to cherish illusions about their own superior holiness, as compared with (to them) unregenerate neighbours.

There is an odd mixture of pride and humility in the attitude to life of the average islander. A subtle balance which is best defined in the Latin phrase, dinned into me in my schooldays for quite other purposes—"mens sana in corpore sano". The great Roman ideal of a healthy mind in a healthy body.

It is, in some respects, the counterpart of the stoicism with which islanders accept misfortune. Like the pilot from Sandwick, who was involved in a frightful crash at Stornoway Airport during the war, and stepped from the blazing wreckage of his plane, remarking nonchalantly, "De 'm burn a th'ann!", as if he was shaking off a shower of rain. Or like the seaman who turned back to get a bottle of whisky from his locker, when his bombed minesweeper was sinking under him. When one of his pals remonstrated with him, he continued on his way with the remark, "If she's going she can just went!"

The use of humour as a lubricant of life in the islands is worth a study in itself, but it would have to be done by a Gaelic speaker.

I remember some years ago reading a thesis by an American sociologist who had spent a year or so in Lewis "studying the natives"—so to speak. It wasn't bad as such studies go, apart from the sociological jargon, but I am not sure she always knew when her leg was being pulled. She recorded one story, however, which seemed to me to illustrate admirably the Lewis instinct for putting a situation into perspective with a pithy phrase—although it was not for that reason she quoted it.

She heard two bodachs discussing a third, who had had a nervous breakdown. "How is John since he came back from Craig Dunain?" asked one. "A damn sight wiser than the man that let him out!" was the reply.

Coming back to the man with whom all this began, I don't know whether the Bernera sailor denied responsibility for the matrimonial advertisement or not, when he was asked to sign on oath. What I do know is that the incident gave me material for a one-act play, which was performed for many years at drama festivals around the Highlands. Few of those who thought it amusing had any idea that it was founded so firmly on fact.

Although matrimonial advertisements are common in some parts of the world, they are unusual in Lewis. The first time I ever heard of a matrimonial advertisement was shortly after the *Gazette* was founded. It set the whole town agog. The advertiser on that occasion was an elderly East Coast fisherman, and it was regarded as the sort of odd behaviour that a Lewisman would never get involved in. For some reason I have an idea that the advertiser had a large pocket watch with a heavy gold chain, although why I should have come by this particular piece of information, and what its relevance is, I cannot imagine. He surely did not mention it in the advertisement, as one of his attractions as a suitor?

There is another mystery. At the time I became really interested in the gossip going on around me, the whole town knew that the anxious suitor was to be at the golf course, expectantly, on the following Saturday evening, to meet the unknown beloved, and walk with her across the sand dunes of Stenish and Melbost where the golf course was then, and the airport is now.

But how did I know? He would not have issued a general invitation to the fair sex! The embarrassment would have been considerable, if more than one had turned up at the appointed place and time. But, if the field had already been narrowed down to one, and he knew her identity, why tell other people where and when they were to meet?

Anyway there were people playing golf that Saturday evening who did not normally engage in outdoor exercise at that period of the week, and their attention was not on the game.

Unfortunately I cannot recall whether their curiosity was slaked by the arrival of Juliet, to meet her elderly Romeo, or whether he was "stood up" by someone, probably male, and possibly plural, who had replied to his advertisement as a leg-pull.

The last matrimonial advertisement I handled, while I was still editor was very different. It was real Lewis.

It read, "Bachelor, small-holder, vintage model, fortyish, requiring slight feminine attention, wishes to contact young lady with view to marriage."

31
They Danced at the Hens' Wedding

Matrimonial advertisements in the *Gazette* were few and freakish. What is of greater interest, and significance, is the changing pattern of the basic customs of courtship and marriage.

Nowadays most Lewis wedding receptions are in a Stornoway hotel. The date may even be determined, in part, by the state of the booking diary in the favourite rendezvous. At the period I am writing of, most Lewis weddings were held in the bride's home and the whole community was involved.

Oddly enough, I learned more about the detail of rural Lewis weddings, sitting in a cafe in the Dolomites, on a blazing June day, with lizards scuttering about my feet, and a thunderstorm gathering overhead, than I had ever learned in Lewis—I was so cut off from the social life of the rural villages in my youth.

I don't know how we got talking about marriage customs, but Cathie gave me a graphic description of the weddings she had attended, as a girl in Back, just before the Second World War.

Customs differed somewhat from area to area. In Tolsta there was a long procession to the church, and, in Harris, weddings were accompanied by a considerable discharge of firearms, as the happy couple were saluted, by gamekeepers and poachers alike, in the widely scattered townships they passed through on their way to church. In Back, weddings were always on a Thursday, and the ceremony and reception both took place at the bride's home. The festivities really began on the previous evening when they held the "hens' wedding", also at the bride's home.

The hens' wedding was concerned with the commissariat. It was no light task to feed the whole population of two large villages, many of the guests being catered for on three successive nights. On the day of the hens' wedding neighbours and friends, from quite long distances, brought gifts of food—tea, jam, biscuits, fowls and sometimes even a sheep. As well as gifts of linen, and other household goods. The fowls might be brought dead or alive. If they were alive, their necks would be expertly wrung by one of the older women in the village, seated in the barn, or perhaps outside it, in a snowstorm of feathers, as fowls by the score were plucked, cleaned and cooked in a large cauldron, in the open, over a peat fire.

The house, the barn, and the houses roundabout would be a blaze of light. There would be a constant stream of people, the women laden with gifts, and a general hubbub of gossip and laughter. The older women were there to do the work and enjoy the gossip. The younger women were there with gifts for the bride. The young men were there because the young women were there. And the children, of both sexes, were there because they always gathered where any activity out of the usual was taking place. No television then to distract the children from the real world to the make-believe of the little box! Even the Nine O'clock News is a sort of fairy tale in which real events become happenings in a story from which we stand aloof.

No formal entertainment was arranged on the night of the hens' wedding, but, almost certainly, one of the lads would have a melodeon, and a dance would ignite spontaneously in the barn, or at the road end, and the dancing and hooching, chaffing and courting, would riot through the night, until daybreak on the wedding morning.

The bride's trousseau would be on show in the house on the night of the hens' wedding, and everyone who came to the house would be fed, perhaps more than once, on the food, which seemed to accumulate and prepare itself in the midst of the merriment—a miracle, almost like the feeding of the five thousand, in which nothing is planned, organised or even consciously foreseen, but happens unfailingly so that every need is met.

The trousseau would have been gathered over quite a long period, but a week before the wedding, on a Tuesday, the bride and groom, bridesmaid and best man, would go to town together, to arrange for such food as could not be provided by the village, and to acquire quantities of beer and spirits to slake a thirst commensurate with the appetite for which they were catering.

On the visit to the town, the bride would buy gifts for the groom's parents and family. Not just the immediate family, but for a wider circle of relatives. Cathie remembers her father being given a shirt, in this way, by the girl who was marrying his nephew. I don't know the origin, or significance, of this custom, unless it was a survival from a more elaborate system of what the anthropologists call "ritual cross gifting."

In spite of having danced through the night of the hens' wedding, the young folk were always ready for the more formal festivities of the wedding night, when dancing in the barn at the bride's home would be continued until dawn, and relay after relay of people would sit down to a substantial meal, attended by a group of young girls, who considered it an honour to be asked to be one of the "waitairean".

The bride and groom would preside over the successive "tables", and each of the men would pledge their good health, often prefacing it with a little speech. I will never forget the look of astonishment, and dismay, on the face of one bodach, at a wedding I attended myself, as he finished an eloquent toast, with a tray of glasses balanced on one hand, reached out with the other for his dram, and tossed it off with a flourish—from a glass his neighbour had already emptied! The laughter is still ringing in my ears.

And then there were the telegrams. Even more numerous than the fowls. Read over and over again to the successive "tables". The wedding involved not only the whole population of the village—or two villages—directly concerned. It involved all the young folk away from home, whether they were nursing in Glasgow, stomping a policeman's beat in London, on the high seas

102

between 'Frisco and Yokohama, or whaling in South Georgia. There would also be telegrams from American, Canadian, or Australian uncles and aunts, who remembered weddings of the same sort from their own youth in Lewis. Or from cousins who had never seen the island, or the relatives they were congratulating, and who would have been very surprised indeed, if they could have been suddenly transported from the sophisticated and commercialised ceremonies with which they were familiar, into the riotous confusion and communal high spirits of a pre-war Lewis wedding.

An earnest schoolboy caught the mood of the occasion, if not the facts, when, struggling to compose an essay in what was, for him, a foreign language, he wrote, "For weeks before the wedding, the bride is busy preparing her torso."

32
Conversation Lozenges

It is surprising how much pleasure can be extracted from simple things. One of the great fun-makers, at pre-war Lewis weddings, were the conversation lozenges. Are they still made today? And, if so, who buys them?

We used to have them sometimes at my granny's when we went there for Xmas dinner, but the fun that could be extracted from them in a small family circle was limited. It was different in a barn, or a kitchen, bursting at the seams with everyone in the village, from girls in the first flush of growing-up to crusty old bachelors who had seen it all, in a life of globe-trotting. The crowd at a wedding was always well studded with "characters", who quite enjoyed the role in which the community had cast them, and were generally ready to play up to it.

"Meet me by moonlight", on a pink diamond-shaped sweet, flung by a daring schoolgirl to a bachelor of seventy was always good for a laugh, but "I love you dearest", on a purple heart flung by the same bachelor back to the girl, or to a tough old spinster, could cause a riot. A riot of mirth, that is.

While those who were actually present at the wedding were whooping it up in an endless succession of strenuous dances, eightsome, foursome, strip the willow, schottische—a fearful programme of physical exertion, packed into a night between two hard days on the croft, or grappling sleepily with algebra in school—those who were present only in spirit tried, in their own way, to contribute to the festivities they were missing.

Many of the telegrams from village lads at sea were stereotyped. The same old favourites came up again and again. But many of them showed a great deal of wit, and ingenuity, in conveying messages which the Post Office, in those unpermissive days, and perhaps even now, might have refused to accept, had they but understood. Gaelic, of course, was of great assistance in this particular ploy, but English could suffice. At one of the few rural weddings I attended (at a somewhat later period than I am writing of), the bride and groom were both from Back. The groom had been a seaman, and the felicitations he received from his erstwhile shipmates were conveyed in a punning cable from somewhere in mid-Pacific: "Back to Back and no nonsense".

When one thinks of the manner in which the rural community in Lewis, and elsewhere, even at its most puritanical, accepted the facts of life, without concealment and without display, one wonders how our modern urban civilisation, in the name of a quite illusory freedom, has succeeded in making such heavy and disagreeable weather of the whole business of sex. Lewis at that time had the same innocent sanity as the elderly spinster in Shetland who borrowed *Lady Chatterley's Lover* from the local library, despite the librarian's attempts to head her off. When she returned it, some time later, she remarked that it wasn't a bad story as stories went, but she was surprised to find words in it she thought were only used in Shetland.

Island ingenuity with wedding telegrams took a new twist when Jock MacCallum, hotelier, county councillor and inveterate fun-maker, from Rodil, was guest at a Harris wedding in Inverness. He was bubbling with glee when he told me how, in the pause between the ceremony in the church and the luncheon, he had slipped round to the Post Office, and sent in a sheaf of spicy telegrams, in the names of the staidest guests he had seen at the service. He then sat back to watch their faces when their telegrams were read.

At the time I am writing of, the wedding did not end with the wedding, so to speak. The third night of continuous celebration took place at the groom's home. Partly, no doubt, to symbolise the union of the two families, but, more practically, to give the old folk in the groom's village a chance to participate. The young folk, being mobile, had already had two nights of it, but were quite ready for a third.

With the wedding always on Thursday, that brought the festivities to an end at daybreak on Saturday, in time to get in the peats, draw water from the well, and prepare the food for Sunday. How would people react today if, after three strenuous nights of merrymaking—and by strenuous I mean strenuous!—they were asked, on Saturday morning, to draw pails of water from a distant well, and carry them over the moor, one in each hand with a wooden hoop to keep them from splashing the legs?

On Sunday morning, refreshed by the first night's sleep in four days, the whole village was ready for the kirking. The bride, the groom, the bridesmaid and the best man went to church together, everything being regulated by custom, even to the order of their entering and leaving the church. After the service, a meal was waiting for them at the groom's home.

Although many of these wedding customs were already on the way out by that time, communal involvement in weddings was probably at its peak in the years immediately following the end of the Second World War, when many of the young folk were at home for the first prolonged stay in four or five years, with gratuities to spend, and the lost years of their youth to recapture.

I remember, at that time, receiving a very racy account of the wedding of one of the twelve Lewismen who were on the *Rawalpindi*, when she fought her gallant, but unavailing, action with a German pocket battleship. Eight Lewismen lost their lives. Four survived the battle, and the years of captivity in Germany, which followed. The wedding was shortly after they returned to Lewis.

"There is a time to rejoice and relax, even in the middle of adversaries," began this unorthodox wedding report. "It was a special occasion to gladden the groom's heart and make his friends happy. HMS *Rawalpindi*, and the horrors of Nazi imprisonment, was a dream engulfed in pleasure ...

"The ceremony was followed by the traditional festival at the bride's home,

105

and despite Mr Webb's continuation of austerity, everything was equal with any pre-war wedding. The moon was in full bloom, and the weather was kind, and the night passed with happy memories of a great wedding."

Then the writer added with a sly touch of real Lewis humour: "The bride was attended by her two sisters, Mary and Margaret, while the bridegroom was carefully watched by his brother Ian."

Despite the unconventional grammar that report encapsulates the weddings of a very distinctive era in the islands better than something honed and polished by a pro like me.

But who was Mr Webb, I can hear the young folk ask? Perhaps some of the old folk too! He was not the most memorable of Cabinet ministers, even if he did affect the lives of every one of us very closely. I'll leave him in the limbo of half-forgotten things until my next chapter.

33
Two Loves a Week

Most people of my generation, groping for the identity of Mr Webb, in the recesses of memory, are apt to come up with the wrong man first. Sydney Webb, who helped to found the Fabian Society and the London School of Economics, was a much more important figure in the life of the nation than the rather insignificant Mr Webb who was Minister of Food, but, while he held his post, the insignificant Mr Webb had an impact on every household in the land.

We tend to think of rationing as purely a wartime phenomenon, but the austerity for some years after the war was even greater than during the period of hostilities. We had a good ten years or more of rationing. Long enough to leave a mark on most people's attitudes.

Distasteful though rationing was, the health of the nation improved during the period of restraint. It may even have been better than it is today. The rich and gluttonous had no opportunity to over-eat, while the poor were assured of at least the minimum required for the maintenance of health.

Not everyone saw it that way, of course. A Tolsta bodach, dissatisfied with his bread ration, wrote the "Food Office," "How man a can live on two loves a week?"

Rationing was not quite so severe, however, in its effect in Lewis as it was in the cities. The croft came into its own, especially when the local mutton was in season. It was during that era a Bernera butcher sent his famous telegram to the Food Office in Stornoway, "Send no meat this week. I am killing myself."

It was also in that era that the Breve wrote the little poem, which worked its way through the bureaucratic system until it found a resting place on the wall of the Ministry of Food itself:

There's no wether on the tether
Where the wether ought to be.
There are chops upon the rafters
That Lord Woolton must not see.
We'll say it was the weather
That the wether could not stand.
It died of influenza—
But the smell of it is grand!

The Home Guard rifles issued in Lewis—American in origin!—were never used in anger against a foe, but I wonder how many of them were used to circumvent the Ministry of Food, by supplementing the meagre meat ration? When the rifles were first issued an army instructor, who did not know the islands well, was patiently telling a group of bodachs in Parc how to load a rifle. He was hardly launched into his explanation when he was startled by a shot. One of the trainees had just despatched a scart* in the middle of the loch, so far away the instructor could hardly see it. "She'll do!" said the bodach, standing his rifle against the wall. What "she" would do for, he did not trouble to explain.

The other islands were in much the same happy position during the austerity period. When the Duke of Hamilton decided to wipe out the deer on North Uist, to add to the national larder and make way for sheep, the Uist poachers thwarted his endeavour. They wanted a continuing supply of venison. Perhaps they were even looking forward to the years of peace.

It was the only period in history, so far as I know, in which the Scottish periphery lived better than London in the things that really matter.

Cathie, who worked during her university holidays in George Stewart's shop, has many stories to tell of the problems which arose from rationing— although most people took the restrictions good humouredly. There was one old cailleach who came in regularly asking, "Did you got cheese?" She would never believe that there was no cheese. She was quite sure it was hidden, under the counter, for favoured customers, despite the fact that the coupons ensured a fair distribution. One day the cailleach walked in just after a consignment of cheese had been delivered. Delighted that, for once, she could stifle the moaning, Cathie greeted her cheerily, "We have cheese today!" "Am bad wis ma stomack!" grumbled the cailleach, waving the cheese aside. "But did you got surrap?"

Of course, there was no syrup. But she had her grievance, and that's always something. How could some of us live without a grievance—real or imaginary? Especially journalists and politicians!

It is against that background of restrictions and austerity the great post-war island weddings stand out in the memory of many. They were the weddings of a generation which had just taken part in a great task of liberation, releasing Europe from the vilest tyranny which had ever oppressed it. They had a right to walk tall, and in those years they did.

While the wedding customs in Lewis have changed considerably over the period I am writing about, the courting customs have changed even more. There was a time when it would have been thought most improper for a young girl to be seen walking through the village, in daylight, with her lad, but no one saw any harm in them spending the night together in bed. And no harm, generally, came of it.

Cathrais na h-oidhche, or bundling, died out first in the villages round the town, and among the more anglicised, who were, generally, the more prosperous families, so that the pattern of decay was uneven, and the custom still lives vigorously in the island's humour.

*cormorant

108

One midsummer night, shortly after I left the university, I went with Ian Maclean to watch the sunrise at the Callanish Stones. We wanted to find out whether the rising sun struck any significant spot in the circle as it does at Stonehenge. We were disappointed. The Callanish Stones are not orientated on the midsummer sunrise. The one thing of interest we did observe during our night-long vigil was a youth from another village, creeping out of one of the houses, just as dawn was breaking. He retrieved his bicycle from a nearby ditch, and pedalled off into the dawn.

At that time I was official shorthand writer to the Sheriff Court. I was seldom called on because there was not much serious litigation. But occasionally I was required to take notes of evidence in an affiliation case. These would average less than one a year—a remarkably low figure in an island with a population of nearly 30,000, and what might be regarded by an outsider as an exceedingly permissive courting custom. In only one of these cases was any mention made of cathrais na h-oidhche. Indeed most of them originated in the town of Stornoway, and the locus of the event, which the lady averred and the gentleman denied, was not a box bed in a black house, but some exquisitely romantic spot, such as a deserted fish-curing station, or the back of a kippering shed in Newton.

34
Cut Price Justice

It was shortly after Robert Macinnes came to Stornoway, as Sheriff-substitute, that cathrais na h-oidhche was referred to in court.

The Sheriff-substitute at that time was resident in town. Had to be by law, in fact. One of Sheriff Macinnes's successors, Sheriff C. de B. Murray, got into trouble with the authorities for his failure to reside within the jurisdiction.

Since then the law has caught up with the aeroplane, so to speak, and the result has been greatly to the public advantage. During the period of resident sheriffs-substitute we had one or two very able men, but also several quite notorious misfits.

Robert Macinnes falls, oddly, into both categories at the same time. He was the ablest Sheriff-substitute we had during my years as a reporter, but he made one or two unfortunate errors of judgment. It was he who was involved in the controversy over Gaelic to which I have already referred.*

When cathrais na h-oidhche was explained to him, by one of the solicitors in the case, Macinnes commented, "A very convenient custom for the local Romeos". The remark was harmless enough, but it was said with a smirk which infuriated me. It degraded and vulgarised, and made unclean, a custom which, in its origins, and against its proper social background, was completely natural and acceptable.

The young folk of Lewis did not change their ways because they decided that cathrais na h-oidhche was wrong, nor did the change imply any improvement, or indeed decline, in the standard óf morality. It was simply that the coming of the motor bus, and the opening of a picture house in Stornoway, among other things, gave them the opportunity of finding elsewhere the privacy they sought.

Looking at young folk today it is perhaps difficult to understand why, in my young days, we were so reticent, but I am sure it is the present demonstrative freedom in sexual affairs which is the aberration, and that, sooner or later, a reaction will set in. It is not, of course, the disappearance of taboos and inhibitions and restrictive social customs which is to be deplored, but the commercialisation of sex. The exploitation of everything holy (or profane) by highly organised and sophisticated greed.

I suppose I got a certain amount of titillation from the affiliation cases I had to record as shorthand writer to the court. It is perhaps significant that I

*In *The Hub of My Universe*

remember them better than some of the others. But I never welcomed them.

The Pursuer was almost always on what was then known as the Poors Roll, which meant that everyone concerned with the case, including the shorthand writer, had to give his services at a reduced rate, unless costs could be recovered from the other side, which was most unlikely.

The result was that, in an affiliation case, I generally got only half pay, despite the fact that court reporting was a burdensome part-time job, which I had been prevailed on to undertake as a public duty because, at that time, I was the only self-employed shorthand writer in town, with the requisite speed and stamina. The job required both!

In the Court of Session, a highly trained group of shorthand writers work in short "takes" of half an hour or so, and are then free to transcribe their notes while everything is fresh in their minds. In a small Sheriff Court like Stornoway, the shorthand writer is on his own. On more than one occasion I have had to take notes of evidence in a case lasting two, or even three days, involving the transcription of several hundred typed pages of evidence. And the task had to be completed in odd moments while running a weekly newspaper more or less single-handed. The concept of unsocial hours had not then been invented. Everyone worked as long as there was work to be done.

In having even the primitive free legal service which involved me occasionally in working for half pay, Scotland was then far in advance of England, or of any other country, so far as I know. The tradition goes back at least to the days of James I, when the Scottish Estates decreed: 'Gif thar be ony pur creatur that for defalte of cunnyng or dispens can nocht or may nocht follow his caus, the King, for the lufe of God, sall ordane that the juge before quham the caus suld be determyt purway and get a lele and wyss advocate to follow sic creaturis caus."

It is not generally recognised, even by Scots, how widely different Scots law is from English. Oddly, English law and Irish law are much closer to each other than English and Scots. By and large the Irish have stayed with the legal code which England imposed on them. Scotland never had an alien system imposed, and Scots law is specifically protected by the Treaty of Union. It is our own peculiar amalgam of Roman law, feudal law, borrowings from England, both voluntary and inadvertent, and a faint trace of old Celtic law, which can be sensed now rather than identified.

One of the distinguishing features of the Scottish system is the wide-ranging power of the Sheriff Courts. We take it for granted that, in quite small towns, all over the country there should be a court of first instance which can handle everything from a stair-head row to manslaughter, from bankruptcy to a civil action involving thousands of pounds.

Historically, it has been a matter of very great importance to the social fabric of the country. An aspect of the Scottish tendency towards decentralisation which was so important in Scottish education, with the tradition of, at least, one school in every parish.

Another important difference which we take for granted is in the office of Procurator Fiscal. It has been immensely valuable to Scotland that we have

111

an independent official, standing between the police and the public when it comes to prosecuting. How much of the inner city trouble in England has arisen from the fact that the police not only make the arrests, but then appear in court to conduct the prosecution, creating the impression that they have a vested interest in convictions rather than justice?

The two legal systems, of course, tend to move closer together for a variety of reasons. One is that concepts which have been implicit in Scots law for generations (at least in an embryonic way) have now been overtaken, both in Scotland and England, by our modern ideas on legal aid, and the rights of the individual as against the Crown.

The other reason is that, because of the shared legislature, English concepts tend to creep unnoticed into Scots law. The degree of proof required in a poaching case in Scotland has, for instance, been diluted in this way. This leads occasionally to a gross miscarriage of justice, as in the notorious case of the Red-Haired Poacher from Back.

35
Red-Haired Poachers of Big Bull

In the summer of 1939, Sheriff Macinnes took a lease of the lodge and fishing of Gress, from the Stornoway Trustees. It was an indiscreet thing for a sheriff to do in an island where poaching is not so much a crime as a religion. He made the further mistake of haranguing a group of young men, loitering on the Gress Bridge, in the gloaming one evening. He accused them of studying the river, with a view to poaching it later on, which to any Lewis lad worth his salt was as good as an invitation. An irresistible challenge.

In the small hours of the morning, his gamekeeper surprised a group of youths, with a net, at the river. They made off. The gamekeeper gave chase. He failed to catch any of them, but he came close to one. In the morning he called on the local policeman and told him that he had chased a man with red hair. "That'll be Ginger!" said the policeman, making two rather wild assumptions. First that the description was accurate, and second that there was only one red-haired man in the district.

Together policeman and gamekeeper—the prime witness, if it came to a trial!—went to interrogate the suspect. Donald Macleod, locally known as "Ginger" was not only the son of one of the best skippers Lewis has ever produced, he was not a poacher on that, or probably any other occasion.

At first the village treated the matter as a joke. The gamekeeper had got the wrong man. The whole thing would blow up in his face. Everyone knew Ginger was innocent, and his mother and sister were able to say that he had been in bed all night. I didn't know, at that time, whether Ginger was guilty or innocent. From my knowledge of him I thought it unlikely that he had been poaching, and still more unlikely that he would deny it if he had been. I assumed that he would be acquitted. Apart altogether from the alibi, there had been no proper identification parade. In fact, the manner in which the accused had been presented to the witness was highly irregular. At the time it was not explained how the witness could have seen the colour of the poacher's hair, in the small hours of the morning. Besides Ginger had a "withered" arm, which gave him a rather unusual gait, although he was able to play football for the Back team. This outstanding characteristic, which should have been much more obvious than the colour of his hair, was not even mentioned.

Things did not work out as I expected. Sheriff Macinnes, naturally, did not take the case himself. But the Sheriff who did found Ginger guilty. He dismissed the alibi on the ground that the accused could quite easily have crept out, silently, after his mother and sister had gone to bed. He accepted the identification by one man, at the darkest hour of the night without any hesitation, despite the irregularities!

113

Even at that stage, the Back folk present in Court did not worry unduly. The real poacher was at hand to pay the fine, and no one in Lewis would regard the conviction as a disgrace.

Indeed, I know of one occasion when a stand-in Sheriff Clerk, who later became a well known professional man in the south, went poaching, with a net which was temporarily in the possession of the Court, pending the trial of the man from whom it had been confiscated.

Then the blow fell. Macleod was sent to gaol for fourteen days!

So far as I can recall, in all the years I covered the courts in Stornoway, that was the only occasion on which anyone was sent to gaol for poaching salmon.

What disturbed me more than anything else was the feeling I had that, behind the voice of the acting Sheriff, I could hear the orotund phraseology of Sheriff Macinnes himself, as the wrong man was being sentenced. Reporters, because of the nature of their work, develop a facility for identifying a speaker, without looking up from the notebook, not only by his voice but by his use of words.

The real poacher went to the Fiscal at once, and told him Macleod was innocent. Many years later, the Fiscal told me that he had believed him. Quite properly, however, he pointed out that the matter was no longer in his hands. If there had been a miscarriage of justice the correct procedure was an appeal.

Macleod didn't appeal. He could only get off the hook by putting someone else on it!

He was released from gaol, having completed his sentence, on the day of the Hospital Carnival. The village was decked with improvised flags to welcome him home, and the young men had a lorry ready for the Carnival procession. On it were half a dozen men, with fiery red hair—wigs, improvised from Harris yarn, from a Stornoway tweed mill. They had an old herring net, with a few stinking kippers in it, and a huge banner, "We are the poachers!" Macleod was given a seat of honour in the centre of the group, and returned to town in triumph.

Sheriff Macinnes was an interested spectator of the Carnival procession, until the lorry from Back arrived on the scene. At that point he left for home, clearly in high dudgeon. The judges awarded the lorry a prize, much to the delight of Lewis.

It was, I think, a notable victory of humour over intolerance.

I used the incident of the red-haired poachers in *Tarravore*, the first full-length play I wrote for the Park Theatre in Glasgow. Gordon Jackson, probably best known as Hudson the butler, in *Upstairs Downstairs*, played the poacher—his hair liberally dusted with a foul red powder. It was his first stage appearance, and he recalled it, with some nostalgia, in a letter I had from him not long ago.

Others in the company who later became well known on the Scottish stage, or radio, were Bryden Murdoch, Effie Morrison, and Moira Lamb, who played the part of the heroine.

The play got quite a good press. It even got a ten line mention in *The Times of Egypt*, for some odd reason I have not been able to unravel. James Bridie

114

came to the first night and was very kind, although he told me, privately, the language was too "literary", as indeed it was. At times I forgot I wasn't pontificating in a leading article. Later, when it was done on radio, with a different cast, Lewis folk enjoyed it because they knew what it was about, but Peggie Phillips in the *Bulletin* found it tedious. She wished it would go away to someone else's house.

The only people who were disturbed by it were a number of Gaelic pedants in the city, who decided that I had got my genders wrong. They thought the name was meant to be the Gaelic for "Big Bull"—which would have been quite appropriate—whereas it was a nonsense word I dredged up from the recesses of my subconscious.

As one of the three evening papers, which flourished in Glasgow at that time, commented, a female bull would have been more Irish than Scots!

36
Other Things to Think of

Before "Tarravore" was actually staged, the Glasgow "Bulletin" rather startled me—and no doubt other people as well—by announcing that the play would deal "with the traditional rivalry between the Lewis and Harris fishermen."

A few days later they got it right. "The play's theme is 'hot'," the "Bulletin" drama critic wrote. "It deals with the problems of the Lewis fishermen,—the 'islands', the 'little man'—as opposed to the Fleetwood trawlers, the mainland and mass production."

There was a further, vital, element in my theme which they failed to grasp— perhaps because of some fault in the writing or construction—the contrast between the official tolerance of poaching by Fleetwood trawlers, although their activities might deprive a whole community of its livelihood, and the protection given to fishing for sport, by wealthy incomers, in rivers which ran through the crofters' common grazings, and, in some instances, within a few yards of their doors.

It has always stuck in my gullet that poaching is one of the few offences for which Scottish courts can convict on the evidence of a single witness. The final irony is that, a few years after the incident of the red-haired poachers, a Labour Government introduced new legislation dealing with the poaching of deer, which made the situation worse.

The new law produced the anomaly, on which I commented at the time, that a man who went on to the hill to steal a sheep could not be convicted, even if he was caught in the act, if there was only one witness. But, if a gamekeeper saw him, with his gun, before he actually killed the sheep, the gun and his car could be confiscated, and he could be heavily punished—on the suspicion that he was poaching deer.

In recent years the commercialisation of poaching, and even the coming of the deep freeze, which has greatly increased the appetite for illicitly caught fish, have somewhat altered the balance. What I might call legitimate poaching is being discredited by greed.

Although the affair of the red-haired poacher was pretty effectively dealt with by the Backochs in the Carnival procession, there were many people in the island who were reluctant to let the matter rest. One of the most active of them was another red-haired Backoch, Alex Morrison, one of the ablest Lewismen of his generation, although he never had the opportunity to turn his ability to personal advantage.

Alex spent a good deal of his early life in America but he came home to

Lewis shortly before the war, and his immense natural ability was at the service of every good cause, and every underdog, in the island.

I got to know him first as the result of an argument we had in the columns of the *Gazette*. He had taken me to task for extolling the importance of freedom in the classical liberal sense, retorting vigorously, and with a good deal of justice, that political freedom was meaningless without economic freedom, which few people in Lewis enjoyed at that time. The argument made us good friends, and his letter was the first of many he contributed to the *Gazette*.

An occasional mis-spelling—generally a "p" for a "b", or a "t" for a "d", the sort of mistake we Lewis folk make frequently in speech—revealed his lack of formal education. Once these minor blemishes were removed, his letters might have been those of a barrister, or a university don. The argument was logically developed, forcibly deployed, and couched in a vigorous, eloquent, and sometimes devastating, style.

When Nigel Nicolson was going through the files of the *Gazette* researching his book about Leverhulme, *Lord of the Isles*, he drew my attention to a letter about land raiding signed "Crofter". He said, "No crofter ever wrote that."

I said a crofter most certainly did. But I hazarded the guess that my father had corrected the spelling and, perhaps, to some extent, the grammar, before publishing the letter, on the basis that his function was to present, in the best possible light, the arguments of those with whom he disagreed. Nigel Nicolson still expressed his disbelief. As it happened, I got a letter from Alex Morrison that afternoon. There were one or two very minor spelling errors, but otherwise it was brilliant. I showed it to Nicolson. He was convinced. Crofters were abler than he thought.

For a time, Alex Morrison worked for the Public Assistance Office, but he was far too compassionate to probe into the miseries of his fellow men, even if it was for the purpose of alleviating their need—to the grudging extent in which it was alleviated in those days.

He also served for a period on the District Council. His fiery eloquence enlivened the meetings, but he soon got frustrated by the Council's lack of power, and by the petty personal feuds which tore it apart at that time, to the extent that my (often verbatim) reports were read with gales of laughter, although they were often written with a sense of shame, and despondency, that my native island was so badly governed, and so misrepresented by its public men.

Whatever plans Alex had to secure justice for the red-haired poacher were quickly forgotten, as was the odd religious revival I have written of, and a great many other things, as soon as it became clear that Britain was drifting inexorably into war.

Nearly a fifth of the adult males in Lewis were in the Royal Naval Reserve, or the Territorial Army. The island had not fully recovered from the immense losses of the First World War, and the *Iolaire* disaster. The news from Europe was of much more concern in the autumn of 1939 than the news from home,

117

and of much more concern to the island of Lewis than to many places apparently much nearer the centre of events.

The Naval Reserve was mobilised a week before war was declared. A similar precaution the previous year had been quickly followed by a homecoming in the euphoria of the Munich agreement.

In August 1939 everyone knew that this time it was for real.

37
The Night of the Black Iceberg

The Naval Reserve was mobilised, in 1939, more than a week before the declaration of war. The first detachment, of around four hundred men, left Stornoway on the Thursday night of the half yearly communion season in town. A day known to me, in my childhood, as "Little Sunday", or "the Fast Day", on which all shops were shut, and all recreation taboo. Some ardent golfers, incomers to the island, brought up in another tradition, resented the ban. They used to hide their clubs down a rabbit hole, at the end of their round on the Wednesday afternoon, so that they could have a surreptitious game on the Fast Day, despite the locked clubhouse and the disapproval of the kirk.

Even in 1939, although there were some small hints of change, the Thursday of the communion week was, in effect a Sunday—a rigid island Sunday, with every Presbyterian church in town crammed with worshippers, morning and evening. The resident congregations were swollen by hundreds of worshippers, by bus, from all over the island. The streets were thronged with black-clothed men and women, coming from church, Bible in hand, when the reservists began moving towards the quay.

I stood on top of the Maritime Buildings and watched the slow, silent, black river, oozing steadily forward until every inch of the quay was occupied. Or so it seemed. But more and more people arrived each minute, and somehow they found room. A little eddy, here and there, marked the passage of the reservists, through the crowd, towards the gangway of the *Lochness*, but there was no demonstrative leave-taking. Just a numbed, resigned acceptance.

As the ship filled, and the men crowded to the quayside rail, she heeled, perceptibly. A whistle from the bridge gave the signal to cast off. Some of the dockers began to remove the gangway. Then, suddenly, from the midst of the crowd, arose the well-known voice of Peter Macdonald, the draper, an elder in the High Church, (a name with geographical not liturgical, significance) "throwing out" the first line of Psalm 46, to the tune Stroudwater.

"God is our refuge and our strength", but in the ancient tongue.

The men on deck extinguished their cigarettes, and stood to attention. The ship's telegraph bell rang. The engines started into life. The *Lochness* pulled away from the pier, through a patch of moonlight spread across the bay, and into the gathering mist beyond. Round Arnish Point, but not, as it seemed, into the familiar waters of the Minch, but into a dark uncharted sea, where she was lost to sight, long before the black iceberg on the quay began to melt.

Dribbling back along South Beach to anxious homes in town, or to the waiting buses that led to other anxious homes throughout the island.

I did not know at the time, nor indeed until one of the reservists who was on board, Kenneth Smith, wrote me from Glasgow, nearly half a century later, that the ship had heeled so heavily, with men at the starboard rail, the Captain had to order them back, to trim the ship, before he ventured to sail. Nor did I know that, as the vessel canted away from the pier and the crowd ashore, the reservists themselves took up the psalm, and sang as they steamed towards the harbour mouth.

The next night, Friday, another four hundred sailed. The same sort of men. An identical mission. But this time there was a Pipe Band skirling, and hundreds of young men and women shouting a boisterous farewell. And so, Lewis, in the short space of twenty-four hours, presented its two faces to misfortune.

The deeply religious, fatalistic, gloomy, long-suffering, but indomitable, face of Calvinism: hard, grey and unyielding as the native gneiss. And the irrepressible gaiety of the joyous heart behind the mask, which breaks out now and then, like sunshine after rain, on a landscape of purple heather, sparkling blue lochs, and white waves dancing on a golden shore.

A week later, little more than twelve hours after Neville Chamberlain told us we were at war, I was wakened by the telephone, and learned from the news editor of the *Glasgow Herald*, of the first Lewis casualties. The *Athenia* had been sunk.

A German U-boat commander had mistaken her for an armed merchant cruiser. When he discovered his error, he swore his crew to secrecy, and faked the U-boat's log, to cover up.

The German Government tried to pass the sinking off as a Machiavellian plot, by Winston Churchill, to turn world opinion against them, but the falsified log was produced at the Nuremberg trials.

There were four Lewismen on the *Athenia*. One of them—Angus Graham from Aird—was badly mauled, when he used his body as a brake, to prevent a lifeboat, full of women and children, from overturning, as it was launched. Another lost a leg.

Among the civilians lost was Dorothy Hutchings who taught me English on Class I. A petite attractive girl, as I remember her. So little older than those she taught that one of the Class VI boys, who later became a staid city banker, got into trouble for slipping his arm around her waist, when she sat beside him at his desk, to correct his work.

She spent five years in the Nicolson, taking an active part in the social and cultural life of the town, as well as the school. Her involvement in the amateur drama movement made an important contribution to my education. On leaving the Nicolson she took a job in Glasgow, then went to Bermuda where she dealt with racial and linguistic problems. She was on her way to Toronto, to another post, after a holiday at home, when she was drowned.

One of the survivors from the *Athenia*—Donald Macmillan of Glen Tolsta—figured, many years later, in an unusual application to the Crofters

120

Commission. The applicant wanted to right a wrong which had been committed by the Factor nearly a hundred years before.

An ancestor of Macmillan's, as I recall it, had been dispossessed by the Factor, on some trumped-up pretext, and the croft added to one of the others. The villagers never fully accepted the Factor's decision because they thought his action harsh. A descendant of the man who got the additional land in the 1880s, asked the Commission to divest him of it in 1970, so that it could be returned to the relatives of the man from whom it had been taken!

While the incident illustrates one aspect of the very ambivalent Lewis attitude to rights of occupation of land, another was illustrated not long after the sinking of the *Athenia* by Alex Macleod, a worthy from Keith Street. When the "Dig for Victory" campaign was launched, he decided to do just that. In a field belonging to the Stornoway Trustees, without waiting to obtain, or even to seek, their permission.

He was taken to Court. Sheriff Macinnes abused him from the bench, as if he had been guilty of a major crime, and added some offensive remarks about the people of Lewis in general, which caused a good deal of annoyance when I reported them in the *Gazette*.

It gave me great pleasure to announce, in the next issue, that Alex Macleod's son, Donald, had been awarded the DSM for rescuing a ship's crew off Norway.

I doubt if Sheriff Macinnes got the point. He was too bound up in his own importance.

38
The Price of Admiralty

When Donald Macleod got his DSM, for rescuing a ship's crew, he was one of three Lewismen in a very short list—an indication of the quite disproportionate contribution the island made to the navy, especially in the early part of the war.

One of the others was Angus Macdonald from Leurbost, whose father was lost on the *Iolaire*. When I wrote his mother for a photograph for the *Gazette* she replied, surprisingly, for a cailleach, "You probably know Angus—the big husky lad who used to play in goal for the Leurbost team. The team that never got a good press!"

I suspect that, although Mrs Macdonald signed the letter, it was written by her next-door neighbour, and brother-in-law, an ex-Colour Sergeant in the Seaforths, and one of the organisers of the Leurbost team.

The third in the list was John Macmillan from Point, who, a quarter of a century later, played a part in the revival of the Lewis fishing industry for which I had argued in *Tarravore*. Having been stranded, unwillingly, ashore for many years, as projectionist with the Highlands and Islands Film Guild, he returned to his natural element, as skipper of one of the boats in the Highland Board's new Hebridean fleet.

For many Lewis seamen the action began even before Britain was formally at war. Neil Morrison, for instance—Llewellyn to his Lewis contemporaries—was radio officer on one of the last ships to run the Fascist blockade into Barcelona, just before it fell. The cargo of cotton, acid and heavy trucks had been transferred from two Russian ships which could not run the blockade themselves.

Llewellyn was one of my heroes as a boy because of his prowess as a footballer and sprinter. His younger brother, Hilton, sat just behind me for a year in Class 1. He also was an outstanding footballer, and the gold medal he had won in a Fife school, when he was staying with his oldest sister before returning to the Nicolson, was a constant wonder to his pals.

Something of the old glow of admiration returned when I spoke to Llewellyn, many years later, about his escapade in Spain.

By the time his ship reached Barcelona, there wasn't a single store left standing on the pier. The port was under constant air attack, by German and Italian bombers. Franco's armies were closing in, and the sound of gunfire could be heard. The crew were dispersed to hotels for safety, but had to return to the ship for meals, and to work.

The only man who had to stay on board was the luckless Non-Intervention

Officer. Britain, and other western countries, were still pretending that, if they didn't look at Hitler, he would go away. Everyone knew that both Germany and Russia were involved in the Spanish war, on opposite sides; that the acid and cotton were intended for the manufacture of high explosives; and that the trucks were going to the battle front as quickly as possible. But, technically, they were not war materials. The Non-Intervention Officer non-intervened, and watched the cargo go ashore. It was a mad charade beneath the bombs.

As for those who were free to leave the ship—the hotels could give them beds, but neither food nor soap. Barcelona was starving and unwashed. Money had lost all value. The only acceptable currency was cigarettes.

"When we walked along the street," Llewellyn told me, "we were followed by a mob who fought for the stubs when we threw them away. A packet of twenty would pay for a room in the best hotel. Almost the only drink available was champagne. A few fags would buy me a bottle. I got a smart new summer suit for a few shillings worth of fags."

His ship spent twelve days in Barcelona while the confusion grew around them.

"One day the order was 'Discharge the cargo'. The next it was 'reload'. The next again, 'Take it to Valencia' or 'Take it to Cartagena'. Then, 'Leave it here'."

The cotton, the acid, and the trucks were heaved ashore. Then heaved aboard again. Half the cargo was burnt, or blown to matchwood, on the quay, while the frantic Spaniards tried to make up their minds. The ship's crew was breaking under the strain. The Captain sat morosely in his hotel, letting things take their course. At last the crew decided they could stick it no longer. They were not on active service. They were civilians getting double pay, re-doubled pay in fact, for the risks they had to run. They sent a deputation to the Captain's hotel. The stokers, they told him, would have steam up by six, and the ship was sailing then! Having delivered their ultimatum, the deputation left and went dodging through the streets, from air-raid shelter to air-raid shelter, to round up the stokers and deckhands from hotels in the poorer parts of the town.

Eventually the firemen got busy in the stokehold. The bosun got the hatches down. Llewellyn, with the help of a deck-hand and the cook, struggled to hoist the aerial. Customs officials had dismantled it, and sealed the radio, when they came into port.

"I broke the seal myself, without waiting for customs clearance, and at six o'clock we were ready to cast off," he told me.

The Captain came on board. A few Spanish loafers on the quay cast off. At the last minute, the ship made a dash from the doomed city.

"The Captain's nerves were still on edge," Llewellyn told me. "He misjudged the distance coming out from the wharf, and smashed into the stern of a small vessel. The other officers crowded on to the bridge. Nervous and arguing. The ship bumped helplessly round the basin, striking first one side, then the other. She was drifting out of control, in a half gale, with Franco's bombers screeching overhead, when she reached the narrow dockmouth. 'Put her ahead, boss!' someone shouted. One of the officers rang the telegraph. Down in the engine room, unaware of the chaos overhead, the engineers put the engines in motion. The ship staggered drunkenly out to sea, with fourteen holes, fortunately most of them small, in her port bow."

When they got clear of the bombers some order was restored, but they found the pumps could not cope with the leaks when she was under way. The Captain gave orders for an SOS, but he didn't give the ship's position. "If I had sent the message out as he gave it, every ship in the Mediterranean would have picked it up, but no one would know where to look for us."

The Captain issued another order, giving a position, but his handwriting was illegible. Llewellyn had to go to the chartroom and get him to dictate the details. Fortunately there were several ships in the vicinity, and they were towed into Marseilles.

By the time Llewellyn told me his story, war had begun. The real war. In fact he had already logged more than two hundred SOS messages—May-day came later!—many of them from ships on which Lewismen were serving. Like the *Rawalpindi!* Or the *Athenia!*

Before a shot was fired in anger, by the armies facing each other on the Western Front, more than thirty Lewis seamen had lost their lives, and four were prisoners of war in Germany.

It was at that stage in the war that H. V. Morton, the well-known writer of travel books, applied to Lewis, in an article in *Illustrated*, Rudyard Kipling's famous line, "If blood be the price of admiralty, dear God, we have paid in full."

39
A Cry across the Crofts

Lewismen seemed to be ubiquitous in the early days of the war. The phoney war. When death stalked the seas, but the armies sat idly facing each other along the Maginot Line.

I remember Norman Macleod (Tomas) coming into the office one day—he was then headmaster at Knock—to tell me about three brothers who had been shipwrecked and rescued within ten days of each other. One was on a merchant ship which was torpedoed; the second on a naval vessel which was mined, and the third on a ship blown out of the water in an air raid.

Around the same time there was a collision between two naval vessels in a congested British port. At the helm of the vessels involved—faithfully carrying out the instructions of the errant navigators—were two Lewis brothers. From Grimshader, I think.

I have no record of the names of those involved. There was so much that could not be reported at the time because of censorship. Even the weather was under wraps. It was a month, or six weeks, after the event before you could mention that there had been a shower of snow!

Only the major events which could not be concealed were reported in any detail. All of them involved island seamen. Often large numbers of island seamen.

Nothing evokes the memory of those days more vividly than the story I have been told of the old lady who saw the postman cycling through the village on a quiet Sunday morning. Clearly he had a telegram. She could not see what house he went to, nearly half a mile away, but as she stood at the door, she heard a piercing cry across the silent crofts. She recognised the voice, and knew where the blow had fallen.

Or the picture of a gnarled old fisherman, rising without a word, in a neighbour's house, and walking out with stoic dignity, when he heard on the radio that his son's ship had been lost.

It was against that background Lewis listened to the news of the sinking of the *Rawalpindi*—a lightly armed merchant cruiser, built for the comfort of peacetime tourists, caught up in conflict with the German pocket battleship *Deutschland*, one of the deadliest warships afloat.

"It was murder, not a battle," was the summing up. Not by an old seaman on a Lewis croft, drawing on his own experience of an earlier war, but by the German commander of another battleship, to a British Merchant Navy captain who was his prisoner.

Although he praised the *Rawalpindi*, Capt Langsdorf of the *Graf Spee* admitted to his prisoner, Capt Patrick Dove, that his own days were numbered, because of her gallant fight. Langsdorf was in the South Atlantic attacking allied shipping. The *Rawalpindi* had effectively prevented the *Deutschland* from coming to relieve him, and the net was closing in.

"I can hear the British warships talking as they search," he told Capt Dove. A few weeks later they found their quarry, and the *Graf Spee* was scuttled outside Montevideo after the battle of the River Plate. An inglorious end, compared with the *Rawalpindi* which fought until every gun was out of action, and the whole ship ablaze, except the f'c'sle and the poop.

The *Rawalpindi* continued to burn for four hours after the battle, before she turned turtle to starboard and foundered with all hands—apart from 26 men picked up from boats by the *Deutschland*, and eleven rescued by the armed cruiser *Chitral*.

It was not the strategy, or the consequences, of the *Rawalpindi*'s gallantry, or the detail of the battle, which concerned Lewis when the news came through. It was the fact that there were twelve islanders on board and none of them had been picked up by the *Chitral*.

There were three close neighbours from the village of Swordale alone. The brother of one of them had been lost at sea just a month before. The father of another had gone down with the *Iolaire*.

The fact that all the survivors on the *Deutschland* were said by the Germans to be Scots, kept a flicker of hope alive, but it was nearly a month before postcards from Germany brought news that four of the Lewis twelve had survived. The postcards were printed in German and those who got them had no idea what they said, but the familiar signatures at the foot told all they needed to know.

I have already described the wedding of one of the four, when he finally got back to Lewis after years in a German prison camp.

Although there were no Lewismen among the survivors picked up by the *Chitral*, there were many Lewismen engaged in the search, including, I was told, three neighbours from Kirkibost.

Some months after the sinking of the *Rawalpindi*, I was told by a Lewis seaman that he read an account of the search in a South African newspaper, which was free from the censorship restrictions imposed on the British press.

According to the report, one of the survivors said that a Lewisman, who had been with him in the boat, saw another lifeboat overturn, and swam across to right it. He was still struggling in the water with the upturned boat when last he was sighted. The Lewisman was not named and there is probably no way now in which his identity can be established. He must remain anonymous, but symbolic, like another seaman from the Western Isles described by Capt George Robinson at a gathering in Glasgow as "the most amazing man I ever met".

Robinson, and three others, were the only survivors from a crew of 36 when their ship was torpedoed in mid-Atlantic. They were tossed about, in an open boat, in December weather, for nearly a month before a merchantman sighted them and picked them up. According to Capt Robinson, the man from the

126

Western Isles, identified only as Paterson, was the only one of the four who was ever able to go back to sea. He climbed, unaided, to the deck of the rescue steamer, and, after four days in hospital, was passed fit and joined a tanker. The others had to be hoisted on board, and remained in hospital. Captain Robinson, who lost nine stone as a result of his ordeal, had both his feet amputated.

It is not surprising that, when seamen were being signed on for the *Queen Mary*, refitted as a troopship, an officer went down the queue of applicants for berths calling out, "If there are any Stornoway fishermen here, they can come inside." And so, as so often in popular usage, Stornoway embraced the whole of Lewis. Perhaps other islands as well.

It was generally of the war Tomas and I spoke when he dropped into the office. He was a frequent caller in those days, often with snippets of news. But we also had long discussions on literature. I knew few people who were so widely read, or wrote more pithily. I often thought he would have made a first-rate journalist, he told a story so well—especially when it was against himself.

The story, for instance, of his struggle to make his pupils at Knock more respectful of school property in their games.

"At last," he said, "I got so fed up I told them the next time one of them broke a school window I would send to Stornoway for a glazier, have the window repaired, and send his father the bill. I thought that would sort them.

"A few days later another window was broken. I carried out my threat and asked the boy responsible to stand. He did. My own son!"

40
He Tried to Quieten the Night

My memory has been playing tricks with me. The story I told about Tomas and the broken window panes in his school, could not possibly have belonged to the same period as the *Rawalpindi*. The broken window panes were in Knock School, but, when the *Rawalpindi* was lost, Tomas was still headmaster of the little school at Loch Croistean in Uig, now closed.

I know because of a famous confrontation at the Grimersta Bridge which, oddly enough, did not result in a charge of poaching, although the suspicion, and indeed the fact, were there. That confrontation I can date precisely, and Tomas comes into the story, although he was not a participant.

On one side was the manager of the Grimersta Estate and one of his keepers. On the other were five Lochsmen, from Cromore, Gravir, Marvig, Balallan and Marybank. The keepers alleged the men from Lochs were there to poach the river, and had threatened them with beer bottles and spanners, when they were interrupted. The Lochsmen said they had been held at gunpoint for two and a half hours, and their car was shot at when they drove away. Poaching? Not a bit of it! The men from Lochs maintained they were at Grimersta Bridge, in the small hours of the morning, to meet a man from Uig who was going to sell them a motor-bike. Not surprisingly, perhaps, Sheriff Duncan refused to believe the story about the motor-bike. He found the Lochsmen guilty of threatened assault, and breach of the peace. The fines were modest. £2 or £3 a head.

This is where Tomas comes in. Sitting in my office in Kenneth Street, a few weeks later, he said, "It was a tall story about the motor-bike, but it was true. The man from Uig arrived when the row was in progress. He parked his car some distance away, and watched the fun, until the Lochsmen made off with the keepers in chase. Then he got out his own net, and cleaned the river."

"How do you know?" I asked him.

"There was one of the salmon on my doorstep in the morning!" he replied.

Clearly he was still at Loch Croistean, on the night of the Grimersta confrontation.

Each side went to the police to lodge charges against the other. The Grimersta manager made his complaint to the policeman at Balallan, in the small hours of the morning. He had pursued his quarry right across the island, and was running out of petrol. The Lochsmen made their complaint, in the police office at Stornoway, later. They accused the Grimersta manager of recklessly discharging firearms. The manager admitted using his gun. Not recklessly, he argued, but to mark the car for identification because the number plate had been removed.

In the middle of the fracas, the poachers, if poachers they were, offered the keepers a drink. The estate manager refused the proffered bottle. He thought it was a ruse to get him off his guard, and seize the gun. His deputy—a local—accepted. Asked in court why he had been, as it were, fraternising with the enemy, the Lewis keeper replied, in a delightful phrase, "I was trying to quieten the night!"

One part of the story may puzzle younger readers. The Estate manager demanded to see the Lochsmen's identity cards! We all had to carry them then, and produce them if asked by anyone in authority.

"But what authority had a keeper to demand anyone's identity card?" asked the defending solicitor, J. D. Scoular, whose office on Cromwell Street was back to back with mine on Kenneth Street. In fact I had a short cut to the centre of the town across his garden. I can see his tubby figure, in my mind's eye, as I write. A placid, smiling man, putting on a show of aggression, on his clients' behalf.

"In many parts of the country Home Guards are stopping cars, and asking people for their identity papers," said the Sheriff.

"Home Guards in uniform," replied Mr Scoular. "If a man in plus fours, with a shot gun in his hand, asked me for my identity card I would tell him it was none of his business."

In the islands, of course, we not only had to carry the normal identity card, we had to get a special permit with our description on it, if we wanted to cross the Minch. The whole north of Scotland was a Protected Area—so called—and subject to special restrictions.

It seemed a little ludicrous that an old lady from Point had to get special permission from the military to visit her sister in Kyle, or Applecross, but we accepted it cheerfully enough at the time. We were not so happy about the censorship, however. All our letters were opened in Inverness, and quite often pieces were cut out of them. Servicemen from the Highlands were particularly resentful that their letters from home were opened, while the letters of other servicemen were not. All of them accepted as necessary the censorship of their own outgoing letters. It was the discrimination in regard to the censorship of their incoming mail which rankled.

There was a story of an officer who found that one of his men was writing, in very loving terms, to three different girls at the same time. It was none of his business really, but he forwarded the letters in the wrong envelopes, and left the girls to sort it out.

The censors in Inverness did not show that sort of finesse. Complaints were made in Parliament that the ex-brigadier, who ran the censor's office in Inverness, employed his wife, his son and his daughter on the job. Invernessians, not unnaturally, resented most having locals, possibly neighbours, in the censor's office, poking into their private mail.

Apart from the censorship, the biggest irritation for those living comfortably at home was the blackout. In Stornoway the lamposts were painted white, but that didn't help on a really dark night, and there was quite a spate of drownings in the harbour. Every window had to be heavily draped with black "Italian" cloth, which led a Stornoway shopkeeper to put the curious advertisement in his window, "Black Italian. Apply within."

As the Sheriff said in the Grimersta case, the Home Guard periodically stopped the buses, even in Lewis, to search for Nazis under the seats. A task in which they were subjected to a good deal of ribaldry from neighbours anxious to get home.

The buses had to nose their way round the devious Lewis roads with a little peep of light, their headlamps masked by a metal grille to ensure that no stray glimmer was picked up by enemy aircraft.

There were enemy aircraft around occasionally. One of the lighthouses was sprayed with machine-gun bullets. So was Stornoway Airport. On that occasion there was a "red alert" in town, and Dr Doig the MOH, racing to his post of duty, was intercepted and held, like the wedding guest in the grip of the Ancient Mariner, by a lady who wasn't interested in air raids, but wanted to know when her boy was going to get his jag.

It may have been on that occasion Stornoway Airport was photographed by a German plane. In any event, a copy of the photograph was picked up, in Germany, at the end of the war, by a Lewis soldier, and taken home as a souvenir.

Like the map of the Ui peninsula, found in a German command post by a Seaforth, during the advance through Normandy. The soldier handed it to his captain, who studied it with interest. The captain was Quentin Mackenzie from Bayble. The explanation of the find was that, on the other side of the sheet, there was a map of the part of Normandy where the map was found. Presumably, the Germans re-used the maps, prepared for the invasion which didn't take place, to serve them in the invasion which did.

There was one extraordinary incident in Lewis around the time of the Grimersta affair. An unidentified plane flew low over a funeral procession in a rural village. The mourners kept a wary eye on it, but plodded on. Then the plane came back. Altogether it circled the procession thrice. Then the mourners saw a cylindrical object dropping from it, in their path. At that point a few faint-hearts dived for the ditch. The majority marched steadfastly forward. The bomb did not explode!

Later the cylindrical object was found to be a parcel of newspapers and magazines, mainly *Daily Records* and *Daily Expresses*, all of recent date.

The incident was never explained, but a cynic might assume that it was the Ministry of Information distributing news to the benighted islanders. At any rate, it was just a few weeks later the MOI sent a parcel of public notices to "The Public Billiard Room, Stornoway, Inverness." An amused, but puzzled, postman took the parcel to me. That probably was not according to the book of rules, but it was too good a story to miss.

41
Swedes at a Bernera Wedding

The Ministry of Information sent speakers fairly regularly to the islands during the war, to tell us what was going on. At least that was the theory. Lewis had its antennae in almost every ship afloat. There were times when we probably knew a good deal more than the speakers.

Some of the speakers were excellent. Some were an embarrassment. I remember one who complained to me about the rudeness of the "peasants", who had failed to stand at the end of his film show, when "God Save the King" was played.

"Why should they stand?" I replied, and he looked a little startled. "When the people you call peasants go to church, they stand at the prayers and sit at the psalms. That's their custom, and it's just as valid as yours. If they sit when singing praise to the Almighty, why should they stand to salute the King?"

He had great difficulty in understanding that it was both parochial, and arrogant, to think that everyone must subscribe to his particular code.

On another occasion Donald Macphail, who was well-known throughout the Highlands as the Northern Organiser of An Comunn, was taking a lady speaker round the islands on a similar mission.

"Tell me," she said, "will these people know anything really about the war? How basic will I have to be?"

"Look!" said Macphail, with a little justified hyperbole, "There isn't a village in the Western Isles where there isn't someone who takes in Hansard."

"Hansard?" she replied. "What is Hansard?"

It was recollections like these that lay behind my little dig at the MOI, as possible perpetrators of the "air raid" on a Lewis funeral. Actually the MOI was innocent. The "raid" was almost certainly a prank played by a pilot of Coastal Command.

When pilots of Coastal Command went out on a mission, they habitually carried parcels of newspapers to drop at lonely lighthouses along their route. Indeed, when they heard that one lighthouse had a dog, they took to dropping bones as well. That little gesture is not without significance. It is an indication of the general mood which prevailed during the war, but which we subsequently lost, and may never recover as a nation. A mood of general unselfishness; a friendliness and openness; an anxiety to find ways of making oneself helpful.

I am not suggesting that we all suddenly became saints. Far from it! But anyone who lived through the war years, and then through the greedy, self-seeking sixties and seventies will know what I mean. The spirit which prevailed among civilians was a pale reflection of what was happening where the pressure was really on, but there were occasions, even in the islands, free though they were from serious air raids, when the war came close enough for civilians and servicemen to be involved together.

When the Swedish steamer *Gothia* was torpedoed in the Atlantic, the Captain had a miraculous escape. The three men who were with him on the bridge were killed outright. The Captain was knocked unconscious. The force of the blast ripped his watch from his waistcoat pocket, leaving two inches of the severed chain dangling from a buttonhole, with a miniature, and a locket of hair, still attached. Eventually eleven out of a crew of thirty-two got away in one of the lifeboats. They were at sea for three days in an open boat, in bitter January weather, before they were rescued by three young men from Bernera. The Bernera people at the time saw the hand of Providence in the sequence of events.

When Angus Macdonald, from Croir, came home on leave he was recalled within two days, and went back to his ship. A fortnight later, quite unexpectedly, he was told he could take the balance of his interrupted leave. He travelled continuously for two days, on crowded trains and buses, until finally he got to Earshader. There he had to get the ferry across to Bernera. No Bernera Bridge in those days! It was midnight when he reached Road End, and he still had four miles to walk to his home. He got to bed at five, but was up at seven to make the most of his time at home. That night he was walking in the dark, with two pals, when one of them asked, "What's that out there? Is it a boat?"

"It's a boat right enough," said Angus. "A boat with a white sail".

He realised at once that the occupants of the boat must be survivors from a sinking. More urgently, he saw that, if they continued on their course, they would strike the "Cleiteir", which, at that state of the tide, was just awash.

He headed for a house on high ground. Borrowed a torch. Then, steadying himself against the gable, he flashed out a warning in morse to change course, and a promise to come out and pilot them in. The first part of the message, at least, was understood. The lifeboat changed course, and lit a flare of rags and oil. They also tried to signal, but the light was too dim to read.

It was a bad night for an open boat, but Angus and two pals went off in search of the lifeboat. They missed it, and, after a fruitless search for a couple of hours, they went ashore. Angus couldn't rest. He got Roddie Ferguson and John Murdo Mackenzie to go out with him to search the other side of the loch, four miles away. Searching along the rocks, in the face of a stiff breeze, they found the lifeboat, at last, in a little cove. It was bumping heavily on the rocks, with no one to fend it off. There was a man ashore with an oar in his hand, as if he had been easing it from the rocks, but the sea had carried the boat beyond him, and he hadn't the energy left to follow it. The rest of the crew were lying in the bottom of the boat, utterly exhausted.

"Ship ahoy!" shouted Angus.

"Are you going to kill us?" asked the mate in a weak, and frightened voice. His back was badly injured.

132

When reassured, the mate explained that they had put two other men ashore, to go to what he called "the lighthouse" to get assistance. The lighthouse was an unmanned beacon. John Murdo Mackenzie ran up to look for the men. He found them in a store shed, under a tarpaulin. When they found the light was unmanned, they collapsed with fatigue, and lay down where they were.

In another hour, with the sea that was running, the lifeboat would have broken up and they would all have perished.

Angus told Ferguson to take the small boat to a point where it would be easier for those ashore to get down the rocks. In the meantime, he got the sail on the lifeboat rigged. When they were all safely on the lifeboat, they set off for home, with the small boat in tow.

When they got close to Bernera, Ferguson went ashore in the small boat to rouse the village. By the time the survivors were landed, fires were blazing and blankets were ready. The captain had to be carried ashore, in a stretcher improvised from the lifeboat's sail. They were taken to the nearest house, Mrs Mackenzie's, where the table was set for her daughter's wedding. No one was busier than Effie, the bride, in attending to their needs.

The injured were left in Mrs Mackenzie's, despite the preparations in hand for the wedding. The others were distributed through the village. Angus, not content with rescuing them, got out his razor and brush, and shaved them. He did it so expeditiously they asked if he was a barber.

Next day the wedding, and the transfer of the survivors to Stornoway, went on simultaneously with the only transport available commuting between the bride's home and the ferry.

"There was a wedding on and we met the bride. She was really charming and helped to prepare food for us," one of the survivors told me later, in Stornoway. "They are very kind people, but we were puzzled by the language they spoke among themselves. We didn't know there was such a difference between the English and the Scots."

A few weeks later the Swedish government showed its gratitude by presenting the lifeboat to those involved.

By coincidence there was another Macdonald from Lewis involved in looking after the Swedish survivors. At the very moment they reached Stornoway, John Macdonald of the Seaman's Home arrived, on his first leave of the war. The first few days of his leave were occupied in looking after the Swedes.

42
It was Greek to them

Although the Swedish crew of the *Gothia* were the only survivors to be given a wedding breakfast when they came ashore, they were not the only survivors hospitably entertained in Lewis and Harris. Not by any means. In the first year of the war, survivors from at least fourteen different nationalities were treated in Lewis hospital. Once there were seven different nations represented in the ward at the same time. Apart from the difficulty of dealing with so many (and often such terrible) injuries, doctors had a communications problem as well.

When the crew of a Greek ship, many of them badly injured by shell fire, reached the hospital, the staff tried French, Italian and German but got no response. Then someone remembered that the Hospital secretary, Angus Macdonald, had been a banker in South America. He could speak South American Portuguese.

When Angus tried out his Portuguese in the ward one of the Greeks replied.

"Right!" said Angus. "You find out in Greek what your friends need. Tell me in Portuguese, and I'll tell the nurses in English".

"English?" replied the man. "I speak a little English too."

No one had thought of that. The sailors had been chattering to each other in Greek. The nurses to each other in Gaelic.

The shipwrecked crew the Tolstonians entertained were not survivors from enemy action. They were the crew of a trawler, which had come to grief, poaching too close to the rocks. That put a real strain on the good folks' hospitality.

For more than half a century, the fishermen of Tolsta had been waging a bitter war with the trawlers. It could be said, with truth, that the steam trawler destroyed the economic base of the community. Feeling was particularly high at the time of the rescue. As soon as war broke out, the government withdrew what little protection there had been for the inshore fishermen. Broad Bay was wide open to all comers. In spite of the provocation, the shipwrecked crew were seated down to a lavish breakfast of bacon and eggs by the Tolstonians before being sent on their way to Stornoway.

The young men of Northton had no doubt they were dealing with survivors from a wartime incident when they saw a ship's lifeboat off the coast, around the same time. The lifeboat was following such an erratic course it was clear that those on board were strangers, and too exhausted to handle their craft.

As the boat lurched drunkenly towards the sands, one of the crew called out, above the noise of the breakers, "We are British shipwrecks!" Despite the dangerous undertow, and the heavy sea, the Harrismen waded out to the lifeboat, and got it under control. There were ten men aboard. Six were so exhausted the rescuers thought they were dead. Four were able to stand but had to be half carried ashore.

They had been torpedoed fourteen days before, and had sailed a thousand miles, in bitter Atlantic weather. Nineteen men had died of exposure in the boats. A twentieth died before he could be got to hospital. Another group, who had been on a raft, were all dead when a passing ship sighted them— except for one, who was landed safely in Canada.

A young apprentice told me the story. "We were torpedoed," he said. "The explosion destroyed both our aerials. We had just rigged a temporary aerial to send out an SOS, when the U-boat surfaced and began to shell us. Many of the crew were killed by shellfire, and two of the lifeboats were smashed.

"We got one boat away with 29 men in it. We had plenty of bully beef and biscuits but the time came when we couldn't eat it. We just drank condensed milk, using the bottom of a torch as a measure. We had two small tins each day, between the lot of us. When we landed we had only two tins left."

They saw a ship on the second day after they were torpedoed, but it did not spot their flares. On the eighth day they saw another ship but again they were missed. On the twelfth day they heard a plane quite close to them overhead, but a mist had come down, and they were completely hidden.

Next day they sighted land. "We knew it was the Hebrides", the apprentice told me. I think his name was Wood. "But the wind was off-shore. We had to run before it, and lost sight of land again.

"The Captain was great. He was a Devon man. By that time he was almost unconscious, but he set a course to bring us back to land, and told us to hold it if anything happened to him.

"We didn't know how tired we were until we tried to land. Most of us had thrown some of our clothes off to lighten us when we were in the water. There wasn't an oilskin coat between the lot of us. We suffered terribly from the cold."

When I saw the Captain later, recovering slowly in Hospital, his one concern was for the men he had lost. "Oh their poor faces!" he said to me, over and over again, as he told how they had died, one by one, in the boat.

The Captain, and the apprentice, were both full of praise for the people of Northton, and their hospitality. Just as the people of Northton were full of praise for the courage of their unexpected guests.

Just three years earlier, before the war, the people of Northton had played host, in the same way, to a party of shipwrecked Esthonians. When I went over to interview them, one of the village boys told me I would find them in the machair, helping the Northton people with the harvest. Then he added, reflectively, "You won't understand a word they're saying. It's a kind of a French Gaelic they have."

I found them, out on the crofts as he had said, enjoying what had almost become a holiday. The first man I approached was the Captain. His greeting was, "Do you know Louis Bain?" While the crew were Esthonians, he was a

German, and had frequently visited Stornoway in the boom days of klondyking. He knew all the leading figures in the fish trade in Stornoway, but especialy Louis Bain who was the German Consul.

Capt Laks, who at that time was a teacher of navigation in Tallin, told me he had gone to Maine to pick up a four-masted sailing ship, the *Viktor*, and take it back to Esthonia. Only six of the crew he had engaged turned up, and he set off across the Atlantic badly undermanned.

"We had all kinds of weather but mostly it was pretty tough," he told me. In a fog the *Viktor* crashed into the towering rocks of the St Kilda group. She was badly holed and became waterlogged, but still afloat. They lost all their food, except two loaves they fished, sodden, out of the sea. They had no drinking water. The crew's quarters were flooded and they had to sleep on deck.

"There was nothing for it but to let her roll her masts out, and hope we would drift towards land," said Capt Laks.

They were in this sorry plight for two days, somewhere between St Kilda and the Harris coast. On the third day it rained and they got some water to drink. By the fourth day the *Viktor* was threatening to sink, and they had to take to their small boat, although the stern had been damaged, when they struck the rocks, and it was only patched with canvas.

"It was rotten and leaky and making water pretty good," the Capt told me. He had to have three men bailing continuously, but they reached land, and were just preparing to light a flare, thinking they were on an uninhabited island, when the Northton folks found them, and swept them into their homes.

There was an odd sequel, a few weeks later, when one of the *Viktor*'s masts drifted into Broad Bay and became a hazard to shipping. One of the Fishery Cruisers—I can't remember which—got a wireless message to visit the scene and report. Somehow the *Daily Mail* got hold of the message, but didn't realise it was in code. The *Mail* phoned me urgently for a story on "the CPR vessel in trouble in Lewis waters".

"What's its name?" I asked, a little puzzled because I had not heard of any vessel in distress.

"The *Beaversheep*," was the reply.

It seemed an odd name to start with. It seemed even odder when the Capt of the Fishery Cruiser told me it was their code word for the location of the drifting mast.

There was a sequel of another kind to the visit of the war-time survivors to Northton. The British Council made a short film about it.

Dr Mackintosh, who attended to the survivors when they landed, found himself playing the role over again, as a film star, some months later. Other local residents who featured in the film were John Gillies, Leverburgh; Sam Morrison, Finsbay; Mrs Maclean, Rodil; and Jock MacCallum of Rodil Hotel.

One day, during the filming, the cameramen wanted to go out in their launch, with a lifeboat in tow, to get some action shots.

"It's a bit rough," said the Harris crew, doubtfully.

"That's the way we want it!" said the cameramen.

When they rounded Rodil Point they discovered what a Harrisman means when he says it's a bit rough! The tow rope snapped, and the lifeboat was drifting helplessly towards the rocks, until a Harrisman hoisted a sail and brought them back to land.

The plot of the film was fictional, of course: a composite of several recent events, including the Northton survivors. The main story line was based on the exploit of Malcolm Morrison, from Calbost, who had been summoned to London, not long before, to describe his adventure to a panel of senior officers, including an admiral, who was wearing the ribbon of a VC, won in the First World War.

43
Six Days and Nights at the Tiller

Malcolm Morrison was only 18 years old, a deckboy, when the *Arlington Court* was torpedoed in November 1939. After a spell in the water, he found himself on one of the ship's lifeboats, with six companions, none of whom could set a sail, or even pull an oar. For six days, and six nights, he managed the boat, practically single-handed, without rest or sleep, but, when they were picked up by a Norwegian tanker, they were still on course, in the approaches to the English Channel, having sailed more than three hundred miles.

Morrison, slightly built and unassuming, learned to handle boats in his native Calbost, but he learned his navigation in the Gravesend Sea School, where he had a short course before joining the *Arlington Court*. Fortunately for him, and his companions, he had just gone off watch when the torpedo struck, so that he knew the boat's position and course.

When he felt the explosion, he raced on deck to his lifeboat station. The boat swamped as they lowered it. Several of the crew moved away thinking it had been holed. Morrison swam across to the water-logged boat, and scrambled on board.

There was no officer in the boat, and only one AB. His companions were another two deckboys, who lacked his experience, a fireman, an elderly cook, and an even older engineer who succumbed to the cold very quickly. Morrison immediately took command, and began to get the vessel into a manageable shape.

While he was still struggling to get the lifeboat under control the U-boat passed beneath them. "It was so close I could have touched the periscope", he told me, when eventually I prised the detail of the story from him. The U-boat commander apparently thought the ship was not sinking fast enough. He put another torpedo into the forepeak.

"The others were trying to bail when I got on board. They were splashing the water out with bits of wood. It was coming in again just as fast. I fitted the tiller right away, and got her running with the seas. I had been with the bosun when the boat was provisioned. I knew there was a pail under the thwarts. I told them where to find it, and got them to bail with that.

"The wreck was drifting down on us. I told them to try the oars and get us out of danger. They weren't used to rowing. They could make nothing of it. I managed to keep her going, down wind, with the wreck following us astern.

"As dusk was falling I could see three or four men in the jolly boat trying to come over to us. Two of them were rowing, and another sculling. The jolly boat was no place to be, in the sea that was running, and we would have been glad to have them, especially seeing they could row. But they couldn't make it, and there was no way we could get to them. They were still struggling to reach us when darkness fell. Nothing has been heard of them since."

On their first night they saw the lights of a ship and lit flares. The ship flashed a red light in reply. It didn't approach them—presumably fearing they were a decoy for a U-boat—but it hung around, as if giving them a chance to make for her.

"We were helpless," Calum told me. "I couldn't leave the tiller. The others couldn't row. The AB and the fireman said they would have a go. They tried desperately, but we were being pitched about by the heavy seas, and the wind was driving us away from the ship. At the end of an hour we lost sight of her."

About noon next day, Saturday, one of the deckboys shouted "A sail! A sail!". They could see a big ship on the horizon with small ships round about. They decided it was a convoy. Flares were no use in the daylight. They had no rockets, and nothing that would make smoke. They altered course and sailed towards the convoy.

"That was the only time during the whole voyage I went far off the course I had set," said Morrison. "But after half an hour we lost them."

Back on his original course, Morrison was at the tiller most of the time. When he took the oars to get his circulation going again, he had the box compass on the seat in front of him to make sure he didn't stray. At night he had to splash his eyes with salt water to keep himself awake.

On Sunday they saw another steamer, painted grey. Probably British. They lost her in ten minutes.

"Then I realised the water was getting scarce," said Morrison. "The sea had got into one of our barrels. The other was half empty. For the first few days we had biscuits and water whenever we needed them. Now I put the dipper in my pocket. They had to ask me if they wanted a drink. I gave the cook water whenever he began to suffer from thirst—he was 65—but the rest of us got a tablespoonful twice a day."

They had plenty of biscuits but, on the Sunday, the others threw the bully beef overboard. It was making them thirsty. Morrison, for that reason, had never touched it.

Monday, Morrison said, was their worst day. They saw no ships at all. But they had one stroke of luck. One of the deck boys found eight tins of condensed milk wrapped up in a jib. It was not part of the lifeboat's stores, and Morrison had not known of it. But immediately, remembering what had happened to the water, he took the condensed milk under his own control.

"But I opened a tin right away and gave them all a little, spread on a biscuit," he told me.

By Tuesday they were all beginning to weaken. Even bailing was an effort, but they had to bail, or lie in the water. They were all ready to take their turn with the bucket, weak though they were.

"The cold was terrible," said Morrison. "I had only my pyjamas and dungarees, and a life-jacket. I had seaboots but no stockings."

When I pressed him on the question of sleep he said, "I must have dozed off at times at the tiller, but I have no recollection of sleeping at all. My hands were very painful. Even for days after I got home I couldn't straighten my fingers. I asked my father, in fun, to cut my palm with a knife, so that I could straighten my fingers.

"I felt by this time we had been at sea for six years. They were beginning to learn how to help with the boat. The thought that was going through my mind was, 'The next time they're ship-wrecked they'll know how to handle a boat' ".

They tried to keep their minds off their plight by talking of the good times they had on board ship. Of the canaries some of them had been taking home as pets. They were sorry losing them.

"We had a monkey too, the coolies put aboard at one of the ports. It would sit on our shoulders. We talked a lot about that," he told me.

On Wednesday, at daybreak, Morrison saw a Norwegian tanker. The others were asleep. He shouted to waken them, and they lit a flare. They saw the tanker making for them. Later they learned the mate had seen the lifeboat before they lit the flare. He thought it might be a U-boat, called the captain and altered course—away from them! As soon as the Norwegians saw the flare, they changed course again and made for the lifeboat.

The tanker came right alongside and put down a pilot ladder. Morrison's companions were pretty well at their last gasp by then, but everyone did what he could to help. The AB assisted with the sail. The others caught the line when the tanker came alongside, and helped to stow the sail. But only two of them could climb the ladder—Malcolm Morrison and the AB. The others had to be hoisted on board.

"When I got on deck I found I could hardly stand," Morrison told me. "But they gave us a glass of whisky, took us to the messroom, and turned on the steam heat. Then it was food and a hot bath, and bed with plenty of blankets. I fell asleep at once but only slept for four hours. I had to go up on deck and walk, to ease my limbs."

When they got to port Morrison refused to go to hospital with the others. He caught the first train and travelled straight to Kyle of Lochalsh, then on to Stornoway, and Calbost.

His urgency to get home acquired a new dimension when the film-makers got hold of it. When I was writing, in the previous chapter, about the film, which combined the story of Malcolm Morrison with that of the Northton survivors, I could not be sure whether the film had, in fact, been made by the British Council, which was what my memory told me, or by the Ministry of Information, which somehow seemed more likely.

Before I had time to revise the chapter, I had to go to Edinburgh, to a meeting of the Scottish Committee of the British Council. When I sat at the table I could hardly believe my eyes. There, in front of me, was a photocopy of the press reviews, written forty years earlier about the Harris film. I had not asked for them. I had not told anyone of my interest, or my query. They were there, quite by chance, in connection with the Jubilee Celebrations of the British Council, which we were to discuss that day.

The press cuttings not only assured me that the film had, in fact, been made by the British Council. They reminded me that the film had been made to promote the export trade in Harris Tweed. They also gave me an excellent demonstration of the way in which legends, perhaps even myths, are created by modern technology.

The film, as I have said, was an amalgam of two quite separate stories, with a dash of fiction from the producer's own imagination. The critics, however, knowing that it had something to do with Malcolm Morrison, who was then a national hero, took it to be all fact, and all about him. And so, Malcolm Morrison, from Calbost in Lewis, became a Harrisman, who navigated a small boat, from the middle of the Atlantic, to the shore of his own native island, and then, when the rest of the survivors were carried off to hospital, stepped ashore, without assistance, and walked to his home—seventeen miles away!

The story of Malcolm Morrison doesn't need that sort of embellishment. The truth is remarkable enough.

44
A Lewisman's Twelve Pianos

The first time I met Malcolm Morrison was just after he had arrived in Stornoway, at the end of his heroic voyage.

I was down at the pier to meet the mailboat, as I generally did in those days, when someone, probably the Marvig bus driver, whispered to me that I should have a word with a quiet, pale young man, sitting in a corner of the bus, waiting for it to start. When I began to fish, and it required some fishing, I had little idea of the sort of story I was going to land.

It was so remarkable that, when I sent it to the daily papers, the *Express* refused to believe it! They said one of their reporters had interviewed the survivors from the *Arlington Court*, but no one had mentioned any deck boy.

What could I say to them? I had only Morrison's own word for it. He might have been shooting a line, although I knew in my bones he wasn't. You're not much of a reporter if you don't know when your leg is being pulled.

I was still arguing with the *Express*, not very convincingly, when my cousin, Stephen MacLean, came into the office. He was home on holiday from Glasgow, where he was serving a law apprenticeship, after a brilliant career in Glasgow University. He listened to the conversation, picked a scrap of paper from the desk, scribbled a few words on it, and placed it in front of me. The message read, "I have just been listening to a British admiral, in a broadcast to France, describing the remarkable achievement of Malcolm Morrison".

That sorted the *Daily Express*. They demanded that I go immediately to Calbost and get the full story from Morrison, down to the last detail.

I went across, taking Stephen with me for company. Before calling on Morrison, I also picked up Robert Mackenzie, an old classmate from the village of Marvig, who was also home on holiday at the time. I thought it might be easier to build the story up if I had someone with me, who was known to Morrison, and could speak to him in the language he learned his seamanship in. The story, as I have told it, is based on that interview. It gives the sense of what Morrison said, but not his precise words, because much of the interview was in Gaelic.

By that time Morrison had been invited to go to the Admiralty to receive official congratulations, and very shortly his name was in all the papers, French as well as British, because France was still in the war, and took to heart the young hero they called "Notre Jeune Marin".

A Lewis soldier with the army in France sent me some newspaper cuttings with vivid accounts of the incident. "Durant six jours et cinq nuits, la petite barfue fut drosse par la tempete ..."

Several British national newspapers had leading articles on Morrison's "remarkable feat of seamanship and endurance," and, when he went to the Admiralty, there was a crowd outside to cheer him through the gates.

Apart from the interviews I had with him, I met Morrison again on the night seven hundred people crowded into Stornoway Town Hall to see him receive the Gold Medal of the Shipwrecked Mariners Society. Later, on the recommendation of Gravesend Sea School, he was given the medal of the London Shipping Federation.

The last time I met him was some years after the end of the war. He came into the office, with two friends he wanted me to meet. He had been whaling in South Georgia, if I remember aright, and, on the mailboat, on the way home, quite by chance, he had met an uncle he had never seen before, paying a visit home to Lewis from one of the less likely parts of USA for a Lewisman to be holed up in. The third member of the party was a young cousin.

They had been celebrating the reunion, and were in the mood for a ceilidh. Not that Malcolm, or his uncle, showed much sign of it, but the young cousin was in an unusual state of disequilibrium. He could stand but he couldn't sit. Every time he took a chair, he began to keel over, and had to stand again to recover his balance.

The whole circumstances: the unassuming hero, the uncle who had dropped from the skies, so to speak, and the young friend who could not keep pace with the celebrations, seemed to typify Lewis in one of its moods. It's a memory I cherish, even if the details have become a little blurred after nearly forty years. I wonder whether there is another newspaper office on earth where such a family re-union could take place, and where it would be news? Maybe not, but I still think I had the right approach to the things that make the community tick.

There were some typically Lewis elements, too, in Morrison's handling of his unsought fame. When Fleet Street reporters harried him for details of what the Admirals had said to him, he replied with a smile, "They didn't offer me a ship!" And, when the BBC Empire service interviewed him, he threw the announcer into a tizzy by wishing listeners, "Bliadhna Mhath Ur".

So far as I know, there ws no one on the *Arlington Court* with whom Malcolm Morrison could have talked in Gaelic. Certainly there were no Gaelic speakers in the lifeboat with him. But Gaelic was in common use in the f'c'sle of many of the vessels, both Royal and Merchant Navy, which were in the news at that time.

When the *Rawalpindi* was sunk, there were two other merchant cruisers within an hour's steaming of the scene, with an even greater number of Lewismen on board. One of them had forty. She became known as the Stornoway ship.

Although they walked hand in hand with death—they might well have been in the *Rawalpindi's* place—they had their moments of comfort. I remember one lad telling me with great glee that he had a stateroom to himself, with hot and cold water laid on. To get the flavour of the situation, as he saw it, one must remember that, in 1939, there was no village in Lewis, outside Stornoway, with running water. Everyone was still dependent on rain water and the well. The lad who told me about his luxurious quarters was living in a thatched house. He had just begun to build a new house for the family, when he was called up.

The ship's saloon, designed for wealthy tourists, resounded to Gaelic songs, and some of the Lewis lads, he said, were learning to play on the dozen or so pianos scattered around the ship.

The piano-playing was interrupted when they sighted a Dutch ship, the *Bussen* of Amsterdam. A search party was sent across. The ship's papers were in perfect order, but the officer, who conducted the search, was suspicious.

"Open the safe!" he said to the Dutch captain. The Captain refused.

A blow lamp was obtained, and the safe forcibly opened. In it they found another set of papers, which revealed that the vessel was not Dutch but German. She was the *Borkum* of Bremen.

A prize crew was put aboard, with instructions to take the *Borkum* to Leith. The German stokers, engineers and quartermasters were kept on board, and worked the ship, with members of the prize crew standing over them, with bayonets fixed.

The *Borkum* had almost reached Orkney, when she was intercepted by a German U-boat. She was still masquerading as a Dutchman, and the U-boat opened fire. When the first shell struck the ship, the German prisoners panicked. They made for one of the lifeboats. The next shell struck it, killing four of them. None of the prize crew was injured.

The U-boat went on shelling them until the *Borkum* caught fire. By that time, the prize crew had got away in the other lifeboats—taking the prisoners with them! The prisoners that had survived, that is.

One of the lifeboats was picked up four hours later by a British ship. The other was for twelve hours in a tempestuous sea before it was sighted. They saw a lighthouse but could not approach it with the swell. They burnt their handkerchiefs, their socks, and their mufflers, at the top of a boathook to try to attract attention. Finally they were picked up, still with their prisoners. Still with souvenirs of their German prize.

Six, of the prize crew of 30, which accomplished that remarkable feat, were Lewismen. In fact the first words spoken as a patrolling trawler picked them up were in Gaelic, "An Tighearna, Phillip Ali". With that greeting, the two Tolstonians on the trawler's deck, helped a fellow Tolstonian to scramble on board.

During their unusual cruise on the *Borkum* one of the Lewismen struck up a friendship with a German quartermaster. They spent a good deal of time together during their watches below. The German was only 19, and intended to sit for his mate's ticket, when he got home. He was one of the first to be killed when his fellow countrymen began to shell them.

That short-lived friendship, between a Lewis seaman and his German prisoner, seems to me a symbol of the underlying sanity of ordinary people, without personal or political ambition, prepared to take friendship where they can find it. A fragile plant which survived the bloodiest war in history, but which is still, and always, at risk.

45
Thirty Thousand DSMs

Although Lewis escaped the bombing the major cities endured, wartime casualties were more than twice the national average. The great majority of these casualties were sustained at sea, many of them in the early part of the war before the country as a whole was deeply involved.

When HMS *Cossack* penetrated a Norwegian fjord, to rescue British prisoners from the *Alltmark,* which had been used as a prison ship by the *Graf Spee*, during her depredations on British shipping in the South Atlantic and Pacific, there were at least four Lewismen among those rescued. Statistically one would have expected rather less than one fifth of a Lewisman—if that were physically possible.

One of them, Donald Murdo Macleod of Tolsta Chaolais, told me the story, shortly after he got back to Stornoway. There were five decks in the *Alltmark*'s hold and Macleod, having come from the last of the *Graf Spee*'s victims, the *Tairoa,* was on the bottom deck. The top hatches were on all the time, but the prisoners were free to move from deck to deck, within the hold. When a young man came down on a "visit" from one of the upper decks, Macleod asked if there were any "Stornoway men up there."

"He said there was one. A man named Macritchie. I went up to look for Macritchie and found him with another Stornoway man named Morrison," Macleod told me.

"Some time later Morrison told me he had been along in the galley and had met another man from Stornoway, a young chap who had once been working in MacBrayne's office, but he was in the after-part of the ship and I never saw him".

Donald Macritchie of Cross Skigersta Road had been on the *Ashlea* when he was captured. Donald Morrison, Newton Street, had been on the *Newton Beach* (appropriately named!). The lad who had worked for MacBrayne, I decided, must have been Norman MacSween, who was on the *Doric Star,* but I was not able to confirm my guess. But clearly, wherever the *Graf Spee* found a victim, there was at least one Lewisman on board.

Surprisingly, Macleod had no hard feelings for the *Graf Spee*. He found Capt Langsdorf a gentleman and a humanitarian, as far as the existence of a state of war permitted. "I was very sorry when I heard on the *Cossack* of his death," he told me. Macleod's views on the prison ship *Alltmark* were, however, very different.

"As soon as we went on board we had to hand over all cigarettes, matches, jack knives etc. Anyone caught smoking was sent down to the water tanks!

There were no port holes and no fresh air. During the eleven weeks I was there—and some were there for four months—I never saw daylight, except when we were allowed on deck, a few at a time, for a short breather."

They made games for themselves to pass the time. They took the doors off the lockers to make draught boards. The doors were white, so they scratched black squares on them. Nuts were used as draughts. The painted side was "white," and the rusty side "black".

Their principal occupation was guessing the ship's whereabouts. Donald had great contempt for the amateur navigators. Even the cooks used to pontificate on the ship's position. One day the *Alltmark* fuelled the *Graf Spee* at sea. A few days later the prisoners knew there was a flap on. The whole appearance of the ship was altered. In a single day she was repainted a different colour from stem to stern. Even the ship's doctor was out with a paint brush.

Then one of the German bosuns whispered to Donald, "What sort of ship is the *Ajax*?"

"I think she's pretty big", said Donald.

"Oh well," said the German, "*Graf Spee* finished!"

After that they realised the *Alltmark* had turned north, keeping in mid-ocean, well away from shipping lanes. They knew they were getting near the Equator. Then it got cold again. They guessed they were on the Newfoundland Banks on their way to Germany.

"I never thought he would get through the Northern Patrol", said Donald. "I was hoping they would catch us, and take us into Stornoway. Then the clocks were changed again, and we knew we were on German time. The guards took their naval uniform off, and laid their revolvers aside. Instead they carried heavy sticks. Then we heard ice cracking along the side of the ship. Our officers told us we were in a fiord."

The *Alltmark* was posing as a civilian merchant ship, and had actually been cleared by the Norwegians as such when the navy swept into Norwegian waters, and Donald was on his way to Tolsta Chaolais. In Queen Street station he met his next door neighbour—James Macleod—on leave from the Maginot Line. They hadn't met for fifteen years, and did not recognise each other until they were brought together by a man from Breasclete, who knew them both.

There were three Lewismen, at least, on another Nazi prison ship intercepted by the navy, and a considerable number among the merchant seamen rescued from Mogadishu and Emirau Island.

Among the Lewismen imprisoned, in terrible conditions, at Mogadishu was Capt Roderick Mackenzie from Sandwick. He retired in November 1939, after half a century at sea, including sixteen years in sailing ships. He came out of retirement in Australia to oblige his old owners. When he fell in with a Nazi raider he could not save the ship but, by signalling his position, he forced the raider to sink it thus depriving the Germans of a valuable prize.

"The raider transferred us to a Yugoslav ship they had captured," he told me later in Stornoway. "She had a cargo of salt covered with tarpaulins. We had to sleep on that. There was a shortage of water. We got only a cupful a day. Our food was a mixture of flour and water—like the paste a painter would use to paper a room. It was sprinkled with cocoa."

On Emirau Island there were three hundred prisoners, men, women and children, including the crew of the *Rangitane* on which there were at least four Lewismen. Before landing his prisoners at Emirau, the Nazi commander smashed all the boats he could find, to make a getaway difficult:

Fortunately the one Australian family living on Emirau, with the native population, had succeeded in hiding a small boat. When it set off to the nearest island with a wireless station to summon aid, there was a Lewisman—Donald Mackay from Portvoller—at the tiller.

The chief freezing engineer on the Rangitane was Alex Macrae, a brother of John Macrae, rector of the Nicolson Institute, and father of Alastair Macrae, who was for $6\frac{1}{2}$ years the engineer in charge of the building of London Airport. Alex Macrae was rescued from Emirau, but on his way to well-earned retirement, he fell ill and died, almost within sight of home.

When the Admiralty trawler *Port Royal* was sunk by a Nazi bomber, a Lewis member of the crew was flung into the water, unconscious. When he recovered, he was given a few days' leave. "I was lucky to get out of it alive, but I lost my false teeth", he told a friend on Stornoway Pier.

"Never mind your false teeth," said the friend, "They came home before you."

The man who had picked him out of the water was another Lewisman, from a different ship, who realised that he was in no condition to look after his false teeth.

In that particular engagement there were Lewis seamen among those saved; Lewis seamen among those lost, and Lewis seamen with the rescue party.

Around the same time a Tolsta man arrived in Glasgow. Feeling rather lonely, he made for the Highlanders' "Umbrella", the traditional meeting place of Highlanders in Glasgow, in the past, under the railway bridge on Argyll Street. He found no one he knew at the "Umbrella", so he went across to the Grant Arms. There he found twenty-one seamen from his own village. They had come from every class of ship afloat, and from every corner of the globe.

When Peter Macleod, Swainbost, was mentioned in despatches, for his part in a mission carried out by the *Kingston Beryl*, he said he saw no reason why he should be singled out.

"I cannot reveal what the *Kingston Beryl* did that day," he told me, "but I can say that out of the 25 men involved, six were from Lewis".

If the number of men from Lewis involved in the war at sea was surprisingly high, the quality of the service they rendered was even higher. Recently I came on an assessment I made early in 1944, when the war had still more than a year to run. By that time Lewismen had won more than fifty decorations for gallantry. How many more there were, even at that time which I did not know of, and how many more were awarded subsequently I cannot say, but the tally, when I made it, included 17 DSMs, 9 BEMs, 4 OBEs, 3 DSCs, 3 GMs,

2MMs, a DSO, MBE, DFC, MC, DCM, and DFM, plus two Lloyds War Medals, the Gold Medal of the Shipwrecked Mariners Society, and the medal of the London Shipping Federation.

If the rest of the country had been winning DSMs at the same rate as Lewis, the Admiralty would have awarded well over 30,000 by the time I compiled my list.

46
Courage Beyond All Praise

Memories come flooding in. Conversations on the pier in the black-out and the rain. Longer ceilidhs with servicemen in the warmth of the YMCA—the old hut on North Beach Street—where, on any night, forty or fifty of them could be found, playing cards, yarning with each other, drinking tea, or listening to the popular songs of the time with—in the early days before their own call-up—Albert Conning, or Stewart Macleod, strumming on the piano.

Memories, too, of letters from servicemen—even, at a later stage, from prisoner-of-war camps. Formal interviews with people in the news, or casual chats with bus drivers on their daily rounds—the carriers, in those days, of all the passengers, the goods, and the gossip which moved throughout the island.

These were the threads from which I tried to weave a tapestry picture of the quite incredible contribution of the seamen of the island to the survival of a nation at war.

I was groping for a way of summing up what I have been trying to say when I listened to a television interview with Borges, the famous Argentinian writer. I am not familiar with his work, but I have heard his name mentioned from time to time, by an old school friend who is better read than I am, and who spent much of his working life in Buenos Aires, who probably, in fact, knows Borges. In the course of the interview, Borges referred to his preoccupation with courage. Not courage for a cause. Courage for its own sake. The courage, as he put it, of the Vikings.

That's it, I thought! The sort of courage exemplified by Neil Macleod of Battery Park, which was described to me by his captain, another Lewisman, Murdo Macleod of Upper Barvas.

"When the ship was attacked, his legs were mangled to pieces—that's the only word I can use—but his courage was beyond all praise."

The force of the explosion flung Neil into the hold, Capt Macleod told me, but, despite the injuries to his legs, he began to climb out of the hold unaided, pulling himself up on the strippings. He was more than half way up before he was seen. A rope was thrown, and he tied it round his waist. When he was hauled to the deck, he waved his helpers aside, and crawled to the lifeboat himself.

"I was in a different lifeboat," Capt Macleod told me, "but those who were with him say that he practically took charge of the boat, giving instructions to the others about setting the sails, and navigating, until they were picked up by a Dutch vessel 24 hours later."

When they came alongside the rescue ship, Neil pulled himself up the rope ladder hand over hand. When he got to the deck, he smoked a pipe, and joked with the doctor who attended to him.

A few days later he was dead, but he had the unusual consolation, in the circumstances, that his eighteen-year-old son was with him in the lifeboat, and was sitting by his bedside when he died. The burial service at sea was conducted by the Admiral Commodore of the convoy in which the Dutch ship was sailing, and Lloyds War Medal was awarded posthumously.

In an earlier chapter, in quite another context, I have referred to the heroism of Angus Murray, from South Shawbost, who saved the lives of 17 shipmates, when their ship was torpedoed in mid-Atlantic. His achievement was parallelled by William Mackenzie of Borve, and James Macmillan of Vatisker, who saved 22 shipmates when they took charge of a ship's lifeboat for eleven days, in gale force winds.

In an interview with a national daily, Stanley Wiltshire, a Liverpool man, who was at the tiller at the height of the gale said, "I couldn't control the boat, but Macmillan and Mackenzie kept it going under full sail, even when it was blowing great guns. Eventually it got so bad they had to lower everything and ride out the gale. Once we were hit broadside by a huge wave which almost engulfed us, but the two Highlanders got us out of the danger."

Wiltshire was in a position to assess the quality of their courage and seamanship. He had been torpedoed and rescued three times.

One of the most ghastly incidents of the war was the sinking by a U-boat of a British liner, outward bound for Canada, with more than 90 child evacuees among the passengers. They were 600 miles out in the Atlantic. More than eighty of the children were killed in the explosion, or died of exposure in the lifeboats, or on the rafts.

Several of the survivors, when they were interviewed by a national newspaper, paid tribute to Angus Macdonald of Lower Sandwick, who had taken charge of a lifeboat, with 38 people in it. When I spoke to Macdonald about it, some days later, he had nothing to say about his own part, but was full of praise for an eleven-year-old boy from Monmouthshire.

"His spirits were never down," he told me. "When one of the nurses was dying, she asked someone to hold her hand. The little fellow took her head on his knees and tried to cheer her up."

Courage is not a monopoly of any place, or race, or age group, but it is not universal, and it is only effective when it is disciplined by the relevant skills. The contribution which small groups of men, from seafaring communities, made in the middle years of the century, to the preservation of the freedom and the comfort which we now enjoy, was out of all proportion to their numbers, or to any reward, or even acknowledgment, they received at the time, or since.

Young people tend to get irritated when they are reminded of these things, but I wonder will the legacy which they leave to their successors compare with the legacy they themselves received from the men I am writing of? Men who fought for a real freedom from a real tyranny. The freedom many of us are shouting about today is merely self-indulgence and anarchy.

150

Many of the men I have been writing about were youngsters barely out of school, but a considerable sprinkling were men in the prime of life with long service stripes in the RNR. Like Colin Crichton of Lower Bayble, who was at the wheel of a minesweeping trawler when he saw a white speck on the horizon. The lookout had not spotted it, so Colin alerted the officer on duty. The officer could see nothing. The look-out was told, but he could still see nothing.

The trawler altered course, and approached a little nearer to the spot Crichton had indicated. The lookout reported that he could see it now. It was a parachute, but he could not see whether there was anything attached to it.

A small boat was lowered but, in the prevailing conditions, it was not possible to get close enough to see if it was a mine. Finally Crichton went out alone, in a rubber dinghy, and, as a result of his work, a Nazi mine was put out of harm's way.

There were also in the group I am writing of, a number of memorable seadogs who had been through earlier wars, but came out of retirement to have another go. They can all be represented by three natives of one small group of villages—Back—whose combined life history would make a book in itself.

They were known to their contemporaries as "Ian Tony", "Bodach an Te" and "Dolly Green".

47
Three Lewismen—and Eighty!

Not many people, I suspect, have gone through three wars, the first in the army, the second in the navy, and the third in the merchant marine.

"Ian Tony"—John Morrison of Upper Coll—was on garrison duty in Egypt with the Seaforths during the Boer War. When he had completed his stint with the army, he emigrated to America, but was back in Britain in the Great War as a naval reservist on the auxiliary cruiser HMS *Amsterdam*. At the end of his second war, he became a fisherman on the *Speedwell*, but, in between times, he worked for Lord Leverhulme as a quarry mechanic. Then he built himself a new house, largely with his own hands, and settled down for a quiet old age.

He got itchy feet when the Hitler War broke out, left his retirement, and joined the merchant service. On a short break between voyages, he died peacefully, and unexpectedly, sitting on the rocks near his home, fishing. A local bus driver, who knew his full and adventurous life even better than I did, commented, "It's John himself that would have laughed, if anyone told him a week ago how he was going to die!"

"Dolly Green's" death was very different!

In the First World War Dolly—Donald Graham 15 Back—was in the RNR. He was one of the first to volunteer to run ammunition across to France, in small sailing schooners, when the U-boat war in the Channel was at its height. Later, he was gunlayer on the *Clan Lindsay* when she sank a U-boat off Ushant. He was deep-sea sailing for many years after the war, and could hold the ceilidh house enthralled with his stories of meetings, and adventures, in far away places.

For a short time he was a river watcher at the Creed—an unlikely job for a roving Lewisman, but, when the Second World War broke out, he went to sea again. He was torpedoed in the North Sea. He was in Montevideo around the time the *Graf Spee* met her inglorious end. When he tired of the sea again, he became an anti-aircraft gunner in London, at the height of the blitz.

When his two sisters died, he came home to Lewis, bought a tractor and settled down to cultivate the crofts of the neighbours, who had no menfolk left at home. While waiting for the spring-work to begin, he took a job as night watchman on an RAF site at Tong. His watchman's hut caught fire. He was trapped in the blazing building, but fought his way through the flames, terribly burned.

Alex. Maciver, the Superintendent of Police, said to me afterwards, "I don't know how he lived, even for a minute. The skin had come off his hands, complete, like a pair of gloves."

His one concern in hospital was that he had failed the neighbours, who were relying on him to plough their crofts.

When I heard that he had died I recalled the first conversation I ever had with him, in the "YM", on the night he was going back to sea from his retirement, just after the outbreak of war. Someone in the group spoke of the risks he was running, quite unnecessarily, at his age. Donald was unmoved. He sat silent for a few minutes. Then he said, reflectively, "It's a funny life, death!"

In his case, it was also a gruesome one.

The third, of the group of near neighbours I have chosen, to represent the Gaelic Vikings of their generation, joined the Navy in unusual circumstances.

As Rory Macleod himself told me the story, one of the elders—whose grandson, incidentally, became an Inspector of Schools—ruled the village with a rod of iron, partly by playing on the lingering superstitions of the time.

"He had a stone with a hole in it, and pretended he had second sight," Rory told me. "Once, when some washing was stolen, he put the stone to his eye and said he could see the thief in the act of taking the clothes. If they were not returned before morning, he would give the name to the police. Before morning, the clothes were back where they had been taken from.

"I was the bad boy of the village in them days," added Rory. "If anything went wrong, I was blamed. One day at the shieling a neighbour complained that his colt's tail had been cut off, during the night. The elder put the stone to his eye, and said he could see me cutting it. My father gave me a loundering I have never forgotten. I can feel it yet!"

The pain, and the injustice, rankled, and Rory ran away from home. Thirty years later, in mid Pacific, when he was Gunnery Instructor on the auxiliary cruiser HMS *Orama*, with eighty Lewismen in the crew, including thirty Macleods, he overheard three Nessmen, reminiscing about the day they had walked home across the moor, from their training at the Battery in Stornoway, and, finding a colt at the shielings on Muirneag, had cut off its tail to make fishing lines! Rory had found the culprits.

I don't know exactly when Rory joined the navy, but he was on HMS *Hyacinth* in 1892 when she made her celebrated passage from Coquimbo to Esquimalt, under sail, because the engines had broken down. It took 63 days.

"She had everything she could carry, down to the Jimmy Greens", Rory told me proudly when he showed me a photograph of the *Hyacinth* almost exactly half a century later.

If I remember aright, that was the last time a British warship made a voyage of any length, under sail. The *Hyacinth* was what one might call a dual-purpose vessel, with a telescopic funnel. When the sails were used, the funnel was tucked away below deck level.

There was no baker on the *Hyacinth* and no fresh bread.

"We didn't mind if there was something moving in the biscuits," Rory told me. "It was the best biscuits the weevils made for."

There was no butter in the ship's rations and no milk, not even condensed. The unvarying diet was "salt horse".

Rory visited Pitcairn Island on the *Hyacinth*, and spent some time ashore. Forty years later he was back on the *Tamaroa*, and the first man he spoke to recalled the visit of the *Hyacinth*. Unfortunately, when Rory told me the story, I did not know of the Lewis connection with the Mutiny of the *Bounty*, and did not ask him whether he came across any of the descendants of James Morrison's shipmates there.

Rory was in London at the time of George Vth's coronation. He and a friend recognised a fellow islander, driving the Russian ambassador's coach to the Abbey. When he had delivered his "fare", they persuaded the coachman to take them for a sight-seeing tour. They had a wonderful time bowing to the crowds, as if they were the royal party! Until they realised that, once they had "broken ranks", they could never get back to the neighbourhood of the Abbey, to pick the ambassador up, when the service was over. They tied the horse to a lamp-post, and disappeared.

Rory had actually retired from the navy before the First World War, but he joined up again, and was made gunnery instructor on the *Orama*. Not surprisingly! He was a crack shot with anything from a pistol to a six-inch gun. In a shoot-off at Comax he fired seven rounds, in three minutes, from a six-inch breech-loader, scoring six direct hits.

The *Orama*, with her eighty Lewismen, was off Montevideo when Britain suffered a naval defeat at the battle of Coronel. Shortly after that, they picked up one of the supply ships of the German Fleet, and took the crew prisoner. They arrived at Port Stanley the day after the navy got its revenge in the battle of the Falkland Islands, and were detailed to assist the cruisers *Kent* and *Glasgow* in hunting down the *Dresden*, the only German vessel which had escaped. It was nearly three months before they caught up with the *Dresden* off Juan Fernandez Island. The battle lasted five minutes.

Later, in Sydney, the *Orama* was visited by the Governor General. After a general inspection, the eighty Lewismen had a special inspection of their own. The Governor General, Viscount Novar, had been MP for Ross & Cromarty and, as he said in a letter to Rory, there was hardly a township in Lewis which he did not know.

When he showed me the letter, Rory gave me a racy nautical account of the speech with which Novar "clewed up" the day's events. I wish I could remember Rory's version of Novar's words, but my own will have to do.

"A few days ago I went into a barber's shop. The barber, as barbers will, began to tell me the news. Had I seen the ship which had come to Sydney, with strange men on board, with blue eyes and teeth like hounds, and speaking a language no one could understand?

"I didn't tell him who I was. If I had, he would have had a sign next day 'Patronised by the Governor General!' But before I left, I said to him, 'These men are fellow countrymen of mine. The island they come from has provided some of the best pioneers who ever came to Australia.' "

The *Orama* spent nine weeks in Sydney. Every Sunday morning the Lewismen were paraded, with the other Presbyterians, behind the Clans Pipe Band to go to church. But every Sunday afternoon they held a Gaelic service of their own, in Macdonald's church, in Queen Elizabeth Street. The preacher was Norman Maciver, who later became missionary at Callanish. The precentors were Donald Maciver and Norman Macdonald, both from Bernera. The Gaelic-speaking community in Sydney were so grateful they gave the preacher and precentors inscribed watches before the *Orama* sailed.

I wonder how many communities produce naval reservists who organise missionary services in their time off?

When the Hitler War broke out, Rory was janitor at the Nicolson Institute, but he was desperate to get back where the action was. His first move was to a job at the Services Canteen, at the steamer quay. It was there he became Bodach an Te. to the servicemen—many of them hardly a third of his age.

Then he joined the Merchant Navy and made a number of voyages, before becoming night-watchman on the ill-fated *Politician**. He told me with great glee of the exchange of "compliments" he had in Gaelic, with boats coming to salvage the whisky, from as far away as Tiree.

Eventually he got back into naval uniform with the special task of recruiting experienced island seamen for service on the salvage tugs.

And so it came about, when the war ended, that Rory, having joined the navy when there were still warships using sail, having been in Crete during the insurrection against the Turks in 1896, on the *Empress of India* at Alexandria in 1898 during Kitchener's Khartoum campaign, and on the China Station on HMS *Venus* during the Boxer Rebellion in 1900, was the only man at his naval base on the Clyde, in 1945, who knew the new naval drill for marching in threes, and was given the task of organising the Victory Parade.

*Immortalised by Compton Mackenzie as the *Cabinet Minister* in *Whisky Galore*.

48
The Crew of the *Rose of Shader*

Kenneth Smith, a Rudhach resident in Glasgow, to whom I am indebted for a great deal of information, recently told me of an unusual incident at Crianlarich, as the first contingent of 400 Lewis reservists travelled south, on mobilisation in 1939.

Their train by-passed all the main stations between Mallaig and Portsmouth, but halted here and there, in smaller stations, for a tea break. Crianlarich was the last stop in Scotland. As the reservists shuttled back and fore between the buffet and their carriages, with sloppy tea, or screwtops, a reservist, from the West Side, climbed on to an outcrop of rock and harangued them in a loud voice. He called on them to abandon their journey, and return to their homes. "The spirit of Prince Charlie is looking down on you from these very mountains. Do not be traitors to him now!" he shouted.

Whether he was a joker, trying to enliven a tedious journey, or whether, as Kenneth Smith believes—and he was there!—he was a genuine nationalist of an early vintage, no one took him on. The incident does, however, raise some interesting questions about the motivation of the large number of Lewis lads who were trained and ready in 1939, and who distinguished themselves, on so many occasions, by their skill in handling small boats, and their courage in tight corners.

They were not conscripted, nor were they carried into the service on a wave of patriotic enthusiasm, during a great recruiting drive. They joined, as it were, in cold blood, willingly accepting the risks of the commitment they gave, but why did they join in the first place? The financial inducement, against the background of the hungry thirties, would not have been entirely negligible, but I doubt if it were the sole, or even the most significant, determinant. The service clearly had an appeal which went deeper than £SD.

Many of them had to go to a fair degree of trouble to get into the service at all. The first hurdle, according to Kenneth Smith, was getting a certificate of Competency in Seamanship, because many of them had no eligible sea experience, although they had an instinctive feel for it.

"It was made easy, in our area, by the good graces of a local skipper," writes Smith. "Roddy Martin of the S.Y. *Rose of Shader*, one of the three long-line boats which were operating from our village, although their catch was mostly dog-fish. Martin was not only a good skipper, but an old world gentleman, well disposed towards young persons. He made things easy by advising us to come and see him. We had to bring paper and pen, if not the ink, and he took a certain pride in issuing the certificate, which was copied from an original."

The certificate attested to the holder's proficiency "in the arts and skills of seamanship." Eight young men from the village, on the strength of their notional service on the *Rose of Shader*, joined the RNR in the same summer as Kenneth Smith. The *Rose of Shader*, he says, had more seamen than the *Queen Mary*, adding, "I don't mean the small one that plied the waters of the Clyde. They both had their share of good ex *Rose of Shader* sailors in after years."

The authorities, no doubt, suspected what was happening, but no one objected. As Kenneth says, the navy had everything to gain.

The second hurdle for applicants was an oral test in navigation in the Customs House at Stornoway, carried out, according to Kenneth Smith, with match boxes. It would certainly have presented no difficulty to any lad who had been through John MacSween's hands in Aird School.

The third hurdle was the medical examination by Dr C. B. Macleod, which again presented no difficulty, except perhaps to the applicant who, when handed a bottle and told to put some water in it, made an unavailing search of the premises for a tap. CB resolved the difficulty by lapsing into the older tongue, with the exhortation, "Falbh agus mùin ann."*

If a story I heard, and believed, in my boyhood is true, those who joined the RNR during the economy campaign of the twenties had an even more formidable obstacle to surmount. In a penny-pinching attempt to restrict travelling expenses, the Admiralty refused to accept applicants resident more than a few miles from the town of Stornoway. Aspiring reservists from the remoter parts of Lewis got round the difficulty, by using the address of a friend or relative in Stornoway, and paying the bus fare themselves. If a cross check had been made on the records, it would have appeared as if one friendly cailleach from Ness, who lived in a little shack on Stag Road, had a bigger family than the old woman who lived in a shoe. And the multiplicity of surnames, among the lads who used her home as an accommodation address, would have cast an unwarranted suspicion on her mode of life.

It was no doubt this intermingling of town and country, and the presence in Stornoway of so many incomers from the Buchan ports, during the herring fishing season, which produced the extraordinary language I spoke as a boy, in the mistaken belief that it was English.

It was in fact a mixture of English, Gaelic and Scots (with a Buchan accent), and some elements of indigenous slang which defy attempts to find a rational derivation. Clearly some of the slang was imported from the mainland, and so was common to Britain as a whole, although we gave it an SY tang, or blas. Some was our own invention, of obscure or unidentifiable origin. Before I was out of my boyhood, we were also using a certain amount of American, newly arrived with the movies, and the movie magazines which we brought to school, each Friday, for our teacher, Chrissie Macarthur, to read.

Some of our usages were just slovenly. The imposition of our own rhythms on other people's words. The entrance to the Castle Grounds, for instance, was never the Porter's Lodge. I doubt if we knew what a porter was. It was to us the Porter Slodge. I have even known of it being written that way in a school essay. In these latitudinarian days (where spelling is concerned) such a

*"Go and pee in it!"

slip would go unnoticed. Sixty years ago it was a major gaffe. Fit to rank with the man who dropped his musket on parade.

Many of my acquaintances would never have dreamed of saying they were going "down the town". They said going "down the vile." It was not a phrase I used myself—the English connotations of the sound were much too strong. I have heard it suggested that "vile" was a corruption of "bhaile". I have also heard it suggested, less probably, that it derived from the Nicolsonians' incipient French.

But what was "hoil" a corruption of? No boy of my acquaintance ever fell in the sea, or into the harbour. He "tost in the hoil".

Do Stornoway kids still say, when they quarrel, "Am no great you!"

"Blone" and "cove" were invariably used for girl (or woman) and boy (or man). One's parents were the "old blone" and the "old cove", with the emphasis oddly on the word "old". I have been told that, when King Edward VII visited Stornoway, one of the Harbour staff thrust a boat-hook into the royal hand, as the pinnace came alongside, with the sharp injunction, "Hing on cove!" I have no reason to doubt the story. A bailie of the burgh once argued with me vehemently that "hing" is good English. "Surely", he said, "It's hing, hang, hung."

Our very irregular pocket money—or, for many, earnings in lieu of pocket money, from the sale of "skeds"—were measured in "wings" and "meugs". "Two wing meug" was a minor fortune. When we were really rich we might rise to boasting that we had a "tasdan". Tempting though it is to speculate, I don't think one can read any subtle psychological significance into the fact that, as we rose in the scale of affluence, we progressed from Stornoway slang, into legitimate Gaelic. Gaelic, incidentally, which derives from the French, and from a French king's head.

Tasdans were rare. What would a Stornoway youngster of today have to say if his father offered him a half-penny—even in new money—for his week-end spending? But even a halfpenny was worth having when I was a boy. Indeed one of my neighbours, a good deal younger than me, was reputed to have gone into Maggie Grant's sweetie shop, on Bayhead Street, not far from the Stag Corner, and asked what she could offer him for a "meug". Maggie rummaged in her big glass jars, and placed before him at least half a dozen different selections he could have for his halfpenny. And that, mark you, was well after the First World War. Probably into the thirties. The youngster surveyed the goods on offer with slow deliberation. Then picked his halfpenny off the counter, and announced, "I think I'll try Maggie York's". He marched off to the other end of the town, to see whether he could lay out his fortune to better advantage.

Needless to say, in later life, he prospered. He had a very successful career, with one of the biggest commercial firms in Britain. In fact, he was once offered a job by Onassis. But he never forgot Stornoway, or the two Maggies who dispensed the ambrosia of his childhood.

Three Maggies, in fact. A little later we had Maggie Jean. A little earlier there was Bella Bovril.

158

49
Where Scroobie was King

Behind the Infant School on Matheson Road there was a long low building housing the conveniences for both boys and girls. The coves and the blones. Segregated from each other by a high concrete wall. The conveniences may still be there, but not, I think, as I knew them.

At the boys' end, the urinal was little more than a blank wall with a leaky pipe along it. There, when we were released for the "interval", a row of ragamuffins in corduroy trousers and bare feet would compete with great earnestness to see who could set the highest tide-mark. Behind them were the cubicles for more private occasions. But not so private, really. As I remember them, they had no doors.

It was in these cubicles the older boys gathered, after school hours or on Saturdays, for an illicit smoke. It was there, too, I first tasted a melon. A strange exotic rarity, although why it was necessary to eat it in so secret and unsuitable a place I cannot now recall. It was there, too, we were pursued and harried by the school janitor, Mr Rudland, or Scroobie, an ex-navy man, assiduous in his duties, and with a salty turn of phrase. I have no idea what was the origin of the name, but he reigned so long I came to believe it was the proper title for his office. When an ex-soldier eventually took his place, I regarded him as the new "scroobie", and was quite surprised when he acquired a nickname of his own.

"Time flies, as the man said when he threw the clock at his wife!" was one of Rudland's favourite expressions, and, when he caught the boys standing on the toilet seats, or otherwise abusing school property, he would scatter them with the shout, "You wouldn't do that to your mother's grand pianny!"

It was an odd phrase to use to boys from Point Street, or the "clabhs's"* of Cromwell Street, or even the "aristocrats" from the houses beginning to spread along Matheson Road. I doubt if any of us had ever seen a grand piano, let alone possessed one.

One of the attractions of the boys' convenience, as a secret rendezvous out of school hours, was that it was completely screened by buildings from the road. Originally, the girls were not so lucky. Shortly after he came to Stornoway, my father reported a strange debate in the School Board. At that time the girls' convenience—the entrance at least!—was visible from Springfield Road. J. M. Morison, the councillor who led the fight for a secondary department in the school, wanted a high wall built, as a screen. He

*closes

was vigorously opposed by the Free Church minister, Rev Ewen Greenfield, who asserted that the Stornoway girls could "stand a good look".

At an earlier stage Greenfield had opposed the building of the toilets there at all, on the ground that they could be seen from the road. They might even have been visible from some of the windows of his own manse. Reminded of this, he quickly changed his ground. He was not opposed to a screen. But need it be of concrete? Why not plant trees? Concrete won. The wall was there by the time I went to school, and learned to raise my hand and say, respectfully, "Please ma'am, can I go round the back?" whenever the need arose.

One Saturday morning around that time, when the school was closed, and the place practically deserted, a girl wandered into one of the cubicles reserved for boys. She may have been the daughter of one of the school cleaners, accompanying her mother on her week-end chores. Anyway, she was spotted by one of the boys, who had an impediment—or affectation—in his speech. In great excitement he went running to his pals shouting, "There's a blone in the plivvy. Come on and make a lush!"

The story was told me by one of those involved, not because of the element of Peeping-Tomery, titillating though that was, but because the accent of the boy who made the find was so hilariously genteel by accepted SY standards.

I don't know what the sequel was. I doubt if there was a sequel. The incident comes back to my mind only because of the key word "blone", and the general welling up, from forgotten depths, of the strange lingo we spoke as boys, and the circumstances in which words which were once in familiar daily use have not been present in my conscious mind for more than half a century. I have been more than a little astonished by some of the memories that surface as I write. In odd moments, when I am not even thinking of the past, words I did not know I knew come exploding into my mind from nowhere, like shooting stars.

As I have said, I was a monoglot English speaker, cut off from the Gaelic majority by a barrier of language. But now I find, as words come dropping out of the sky, that I had a much greater Gaelic vocabulary than I have always believed. Certainly a much greater Gaelic vocabulary than I was aware of, when I actually used these Gaelic words.

I find, as I recall them, that they fell into well defined groups. Some I recognised as Gaelic at the time I used them, and I used them with a certain amount of bravado, or showing off. But many of them were not recognised for what they were. I used them as if they were English, or Stornoway slang. Some were distorted or misapplied.

I also used, and still do, a great many Gaelic constructions without recognising that they are solecisms in English. Sometimes, when Cathie points out to me jocularly that I have used a Gaelic, rather than an English, construction, I persist in using it, because I feel it gives a shade of meaning I would find it difficult to convey in strict grammatical English. Sometimes I persist because the habit of misuse is so deeply engrained I cannot break it off.

It is interesting that a true bi-lingual speaker can keep the languages in separate compartments. It is the monoglot English-speaker, who came under

160

Gaelic influence in his youth without acquiring the language, who has had his English corrupted by the touch.

The relationship might have been different in a better ordered society. English could have borrowed from Gaelic with great advantage, just as Gaelic must necessarily borrow from English. The trouble arises when there is a difference in status between two neighbouring languages. Then the weaker language borrows unnecessarily, and borrows the wrong things, while the stronger strives to suppress, or conceal, the borrowings it has made.

Any living language borrows what it needs. A language is no longer living—or is in danger of no longer living—when it borrows what it could supply from its own resources. I am sometimes appalled by the bastard Gaelic used by educated people. Even by those responsible for the education of others. There is something far wrong when the fact that their vocabulary is misbegotten is obvious even to an English-speaker like myself. Murdo Macfarlane was right when he used to lament the squandering, by a foolish generation, of the great riches of the Gaelic vocabulary, which had still been in common use in their youth.

One should either take pride in the language, or give it a decent burial. And taking pride in the language does not mean talking big about it, or doing stupid, aggressive and counter-productive things. It means engaging in the hard slog of disentangling one's Gaelic vocabulary from English. Recovering what has been lost, and finding viable words and phrases for the things that lie outside the old tradition. Having the attitude to Gaelic that the Elizabethans had to English. The creative frenzy of word-making that gave us Shakespeare, Milton, Marlowe, and the Authorised Version of the Bible.

I have always envied those who were equipped to labour in this difficult field, and who have laboured in it with considerable success. At the same time I have never been blind to the danger of creating a too tightly enclosed community. An aggressive Gaelic nationalism (or parochialism) defending its own absurdity.

While people like Sorley MacLean, Derick Thomson, Iain Crichton Smith, Donald Macaulay, Finlay Macleod, John Murray, D. J. Mackay, Fred Macaulay, and others, are recreating Gaelic as a powerful cultural tool, those who paint slogans, and deface road signs, are avoiding the heat and burden of the battle to pursue a political will-o-the wisp at little or no cost to themselves.

Protest is the reaction of the baby who screams because it hasn't the ability to do anything else. Creation is the highest activity of which man is capable. And it takes sweat.

50
The Fish Spoke Gaelic

Around the harbour, in particular, Gaelic predominated in my youth. In fact when, as students at Glasgow University, we discussed a Gaelic menu for the centenary dinner of the Ossianic Society, the two monoglot English-speakers from Stornoway—Stephen MacLean and myself—found, to our surprise, that we were more familiar with the Gaelic names of the edible fish than many native Gaelic-speakers from the other islands.

A herring was always "sgadan", except when it was abbreviated to "sked". Fresh herring was "sgadan ur", which is not surprising, because that was the cry of the carters as they hawked from door to door the finest food in the world. My favourite form of fresh herring was split and fried in oatmeal. What I would call, rightly or wrongly, a "spealtaireach", quite spontaneously. I was familiar with the Scots "spelding" but it did not come so trippingly to the tongue.

Salt herring were different. I never spoke of a salt herring as 'sgadan saillte". But then, they weren't hawked from door to door. There was no carters' call to prompt me. Every family salted its own winter supply, or bought a half barrel, or a firkin, from a curer. That was the one area in which we conceded the superiority of Loch Fyne herring to our own. They were smaller and, when cured, more delicate than the whopping fish that came from the Minch. With kippers it was different. We wouldn't take Loch Fyne kippers in a gift.

Mackerel was the odd man out in our use of Gaelic. I would never have called a mackerel, "runnach", although no doubt I could have found the word if I had rummaged the recesses of my mind. A mackerel was always a "mog". Fit only to use as bait for worthier species. The change which has come over the status of the mackerel in recent years is one of the wonders of my life—a French Revolution of the sea. Or of the dinner table. We thought the mackerel a dirty fish. Too strongly flavoured. Highly perishable. We ate it on rare occasions, when other fish were unobtainable, but only if it was mint fresh, with the sea water hardly dry on its back. Every summer a group of small Swedish fishing vessels anchored in Glumaig Bay. They didn't fish. They bought the mackerel accidentally caught by the herring drifters. They were a drug on the market. Going cheap. The Swedes roused them on board, and departed with a profitable catch, without having put a net in the sea. Smoked mackerel! As a child the very idea would have made me puke. Now it's a gourmet's delight. My gourmet's delight.

Scampi has come up in the world in the same way. The first time I tasted scampi I got a sackful, free, from a trawler. They were a by-catch the crew didn't want to know about. Twenty or thirty years later they were an important article of commerce, engaging the attention of a committee in St Andrew's House, at whose meeting I was rather baffled, until I realised that the man who spoke about scampi, the man who spoke about Norway lobsters, and the man who spoke about Dublin Bay prawns, all meant the same thing, although they appeared to have some difficulty in saying so.

As a child I never fished for pollack or trosg, although I knew that trosg was cod. But then I never fished for cod either. I fished for bodach-ruadhs, giving an English plural to a Gaelic singular. A difficulty I avoided (unconsciously) with herring, where the plural of sgadan, for me, was skeds.

I would never have called a crab a partan, much less a duine dreamach, which are the names Maclennan gives in the English-Gaelic section of his dictionary. Invariably I would speak of a crubag, which, I was interested to see, he does give in the Gaelic-English section.

When we used to catch flat fish with our feet, on the in-coming tide at the Cockle-ebb, we didn't call them flounders. They were always flukes or leòbags. Again the intrusive English plural. I still think there is nothing tastier than a leòbag, fresh from Broad Bay, in its season—unless it is a wing of skate. A fish which caused me no problems because the sound is much the same in both languages.

Perhaps the best illustration of the supremacy of Gaelic, for an English-speaking boy, around the wharves in Stornoway, in the first quarter of the century, is provided by the fish of which I didn't know the English name. I can see them now, quite vividly, flapping their hearts out at my feet, on the tarred boards of the steamer quay, which vanished nearly half a century ago. Big compared with the cuddies we normally caught. Glowing red beneath the scales. An oddly shaped creature that looked like a flat fish, swimming on its edge. A real exotic, for whose arrival we waited with interest at the appropriate season. Undoubtedly it was the carbhanach. That name I know, with every fibre in my body still responding to a childish thrill. But what on earth is the English name? There I have to grope. Surely it was bream? Or was it?

I looked up Maclennan and found that, in the Gaelic-English section, he translates carbhanach simply as carp. In the English-Gaelic section bream is not listed at all. At that point I turned to the encyclopaedia, which confirmed my idea that carp is purely a fresh water fish. We certainly did not catch carp from the point of Number One Pier. The encyclopaedia did, however, tell me that while bream is also a fresh water fish, the name is applied to some salt water species illustrated on another page. I turned to the page indicated, and there was the Black Bream, which "provides sport for anglers off the English coast in summer". The right shape for my carbhanach, and the right reputation, but the wrong colour. But then there was a mention of the Red Bream, which was not illustrated, but was surely what I was looking for.

When we called the Red Bream carbhanach, as children, were we drawing an analogy of our own, or has the word a wider meaning than Maclennan allows?

No matter. Let me stay with Maclennan's carbhanach—the carp. I have heard it said that there are carp in Loch Orasay, which were introduced many centuries ago by the monks. I cannot vouch for the manner in which the carp were introduced: I presume it is merely a historian's guess. Nor can I vouch for their existence. I have never had the time or patience to be an angler, and haven't put the matter to the test.

But I was told once, in rather unusual circumstances, that there are carp in another Lewis loch, somewhere in Parc. The information was given to me by a very able councillor, who invaded my office, in an advanced state of intoxication. I found it impossible to get rid of him, although it was long past my mealtime, but I felt I was rewarded, marginally at least, when he mentioned the carp.

"They're almost impossible to catch," he assured me. "There's no use trying bait or fly. You have to wait till they jump and shoot the b...s!"

That would be pretty good marksmanship—even for a poacher from Parc.

51
Lewis Prime Minister and London Prostitutes

I have been trying to think back to the source of the Gaelic words I used as a child. The names of the fish would have come from my playmates, but the other words I used did not. As far as I can recall, I picked them up in the home, mainly from my mother, and not so much from her conversation with me, as from overhearing her conversation with her friends. So, presumably they represented a fairly established pattern among SY's of that generation.

How often have I been told not to be so rapach, when I failed to tidy my clothes away in the bedroom, or left my toys scattered around? How often have I gone sporghailing, for matches, in the dark, when I wanted to light my bedside candle? Matches were scarce. Lighters unknown. We always had a jar of spills, made from folded newspaper strips, so that we could light the candles, or the lamps, from the fire. But there was no fire in the bedroom. No heating of any sort, until the paraffin stove came into use, when I was in my teens.

The intrusive suffix shows that sporghail had been absorbed into our English vocabulary with many other Gaelic words. My knife was always a sgian. It sounded more romantic. Mrs Maclennan's hens roosted on a spiris. I doubt whether I knew the word perch as a child. We also applied the word spiris, jocularly, to the pulpit in church. If we thought a minister pompous, we might say he had a good beachd of himself, and refer to his antics on the spiris.

When I started playing golf as a youngster there were still little metal boxes of damp sand on every tee, from which we took a pinch to make a little sand castle, for the ball to sit on. But, when the wooden peg came in, we generally referred to it as the spidean.

A hen was a cearc and a cockerel a coileach, but I did not always distinguish clearly enough between coileach and cailleach, which was confusing. My brother, when he was very young, confused the two in a physical rather than a linguistic sense. He answered the door-bell, and hurried into the kitchen, announcing to my mother in a loud voice, which the visitor must have heard, "There's a woman at the door with a face like a hen." When my mother went to the door, her embarrassment was increased by the fact that she found his description was an apt one.

I don't know what my mother said to him afterwards, but she might well have asked him "What brath did you take to the poor woman, when you called her a hen?". Taking a brath to, or on, someone was a phrase frequently used among my mother's friends.

I have discovered in conversation with Cathie that I and my childhood pals sometimes extended the Gaelic words we used well beyond their proper meaning. She would use smid only in the context of conversation. "He didn't say a smid about it!" I would say things like, "The house was so tidy you couldn't see a smid of dust anywhere."

I don't know whether there is anything to be learned from the use and abuse of Gaelic by English speakers in SY in my childhood, but it has certainly provided us with an interesting topic of conversation over recent weeks. One evening, when we were on the subject, the TV gave a sharp crack and the screen went blank.

"What a brac!" said Cathie. "Would you have used that word as a child?"

"My childhood was punctuated with bracs," I replied. "I would have used nothing else for a noise like that. The mystery is why I dispensed with the use of so serviceable a word. I can think of no precise equivalent in English."

The reference to my childhood brought to my mind the fact, previously overlooked, that the programme we had been watching had its own associations with the Gaelic-English, incomer-native pattern of the Lewis community. It was the first of the ITV series "Number Ten", about Gladstone, and his nocturnal mission among the prostitutes of London, which his colleagues feared might bring the government down, if the news of his wanderings leaked out.

I picked up the Dictionary of National Biography and looked up the relevant entry. "Gladstone, William Ewart, statesman and author, born 20th December, 1809, at 62 Rodney Street, Liverpool, fourth son of Sir John Gladstone and his second wife, Anne, daughter of Andrew Robertson, of Stornoway."

Gladstone boasted during his Midlothian campaign that there was not a drop of blood in his veins which was not Scottish. His mother was born in Stornoway, although the family later moved to Dingwall where her father was provost for a record period of twenty years. In September 1883, when Gladstone, then at the height of his fame, was travelling to Copenhagen to meet the Tzar and other European rulers, Sir Donald Currie's yacht, the *Pembroke Castle*, on which he was sailing, stopped in the mouth of Stornoway Harbour. Gladstone had no time to go ashore, but he wanted to have, at least, a look at the town where his mother was born. Standing with him on the bridge was a very old friend, the poet Tennyson.

During the Midlothian campaign, Gladstone's speeches were avidly followed by a young Lewis minister, Rev Norman C. Macfarlane, from Crobeg, whom I have already mentioned in another context. In his rather florid way, Macfarlane later wrote, "Lewismen who heard Mr Gladstone felt a thrill at his Lewis blood ... He inherited (as far as heredity is concerned in these things) his spiritual instincts and religious tendencies, not from his finely gifted father, but from his devout and Godly mother. Lewis Christianity made him a dissenter, and put iron into her son's blood."

If it was his Lewis inheritance which so disturbed the statesman's nights that he went prowling through the streets of London, to the consternation of his colleagues, bequeathing to us one of the great enigmas of Victorian morality, perhaps we have more to answer for than we care to admit.

I was just on the point of writing that Macfarlane had overplayed the Lewis influence on Gladstone's mother, when I remembered a passage in the memoirs of Evander Maciver of Gress, who knew her personally, and was related to her by marriage.

"She was a woman of very high character, talents and piety, with a fine presence," he wrote of this Lewis lady, who has found her way into the history books as the mother of three MPs, one of them a great Prime Minister. "It must have been from her that he inherited and acquired such nobility of character and conduct."

Evander Maciver spent a week with Gladstone at Lochinver, where they had a long discussion on Highland superstition. The statesman thought Maciver was pulling his leg when he said people still believed cows could be deprived of their milk by a neighbour's evil eye.

Next day, when they were out walking, they met a crofter. Maciver asked him whether he believed in the evil eye. "Yes!" was the reply. "Just as surely as you do!"

Gladstone was so surprised he told the story at breakfast, as a joke, and discovered that all the ladies present agreed with the crofter. It must have given him a jolt to discover that supersition has nothing to do with class.

Although his connection with Lewis was rather tenuous, Gladstone did correspond with at least one of his Lewis relatives: John Mackenzie, of the firm of Mackenzie and Macfarlane, whose shop I remember, somewhat vaguely. I would place it on Point Street, in the property now owned by Charles Morrison & Son Ltd.

And certainly Gladstone acknowledged his debt to his Lewis mother, whom he described as "a beautiful and admirable woman."

I can think of many more Lewis mothers to whom these adjectives could be applied.

52
Surprises Still in Store

When Gladstone entered Parliament, just after the passing of the great Reform Act of 1832, he was a conservative. He had been opposed to the Act. His progress towards liberalism was slow and deliberate. His early speeches were often quoted against him by opponents, as if there was no learning process in life. No scope for illumination. Or conversion.

His maiden speech in the House of Commons was made in defence of his father's record as a slave owner in Demarara. It has a special interest for us. The future Prime Minister, whose mother was born in Lewis, was replying, in effect, to another great reformer, whose father was born in Harris. Both the protagonists, in this confrontation of the islands, if I may call it so, were later accorded the ultimate accolade. They were buried in Westminster Abbey.

Gladstone did not condone slavery, but he wanted the process of emancipation to be gradual. He was replying to the attacks on the plantation owners, maintained by the formidable anti-slavery lobby in both Houses of Parliament. According to Charles Booth "the whole of the data for every one of the anti-slavery speeches" was supplied by Zachary Macaulay. Zachary was the son of Rev John Macaulay, who was born in Harris, where his father was minister for many years. John was a direct descendant of the notorious Domhnull Cam, and his equally notorious enemy, the last of the Morison Breves of Lewis.

Like his, even more famous, son, Lord Macaulay the historian, Zachary had a most retentive memory. He was one of the first scientific social investigators. A brilliant statistician. And, among the leaders of the movement he was the only one who could speak of conditions in the slave trade from direct observation, both in the West Indies and in Africa. When Wilberforce, the leader of the movement, was stuck for information, or ammunition, his cry was, "Look it up in Macaulay!"

In one of the key debates in British social history, dealing with a great moral issue, two of the leading figures were just one generation removed from the Outer Hebrides. They were not diametrically opposed to each other. Each had a positive, and massive, contribution to make to reform. More importantly for us, perhaps, they were both in process of being absorbed into the English establishment. Gladstone himself, in spite of his Midlothian speeches, and Zachary's son, are now regarded as quintessential Englishmen.

One of my recurring themes has been that the islands are not a closed community. There is always an interchange of people and ideas. But, while the inflow has been small, intermittent, and generally temporary, so far as people are concerned, the outflow has been large, continuous and generally permanent. We gained for a few years, or at most for a couple of generations, the Robertsons from whom Gladstone was descended. Members of the family have appeared, and will appear from time to time, in these reminiscences. They played an important part in the life of the community while they were of it. But, once the family had moved to the wider stage, a passing look at the island, as their ship steamed through the Minch, was the extent of their interest.

Although this is ancient history, in a sense, it is highly relevant to what is happening in the islands today. It is the leeching away of ability over the centuries, and the debilitating effect this had on the life of the community, which makes the current attempt to build up, from within, and retain a higher proportion of the islands' ablest sons and daughters at home, so exciting, and so important. The disbalance between losses and gains at the point of contact with the outside world is the mirror image of what was happening in regard to language. English borrowings from Gaelic, as exemplified by the vocabulary of my childhood, were limited, inaccurate and temporary. The borrowings from English by Gaelic-speakers, in the same period, were extensive, demoralising and permanent. Permanent, that is, unless the trend is reversed by a concious effort of the collective will.

It would be interesting to have a list of the English words which have passed, unnecessarily, into colloquial Gaelic speech in the past seventy years—and the good Gaelic words they have replaced—to match the list of Gaelic words which temporarily enriched the vocabulary of English-speaking Stornowegians in my childhood.

I was often accused of being rù rà, or greannach, or busach. The Loch Fyne fishermen were always Deasachs. Breug a rithist was a phrase I heard frequently used by my mother, and my aunts, when exchanging the local gossip, but it shows the state of ignorance in which I languished that I always thought it meant a particularly vicious or outrageous liar. I had no idea it referred to the lie, rather than to the person who uttered it.

I would call my shoes brògan, using a Gaelic plural for once, but I would only use the word humorously, and conscious that I was borrowing from the other tongue. I would never call my shoes brogues. That was the name of a specific type of shoe. My trousers, on the other hand—or should I say the other leg—were almost always briogais. Sometimes my mother would refer to them as "briogais a bh' air Alasdair," which I took to be a snatch from a popular song, but I never knew, or enquired, who Alasdair was, or what was special about his trousers.

Ceann cropic I was inordinately fond of. I still am. I was familiar with the name crappit heid but would not have used it. Whether there is an English name for this noble dish I do not really know, but ceann cropic and crappit heid are words to warm the heart, or at any rate set the gastric juices flowing.

Ceann I would use quite naturally for my head, but never lamh for my hand. And cas for my foot, only when I wanted to be funny. I was familiar enough with the word, and some of its specialised uses, to enjoy the story of the occasion when Stephen's father found his newly acquired car getting out of control, on a steep brae, and his Uig cousin told him urgently to "put her in the cas bheag!".

Bayhead was always Ceann a Bhàigh. I liked a copan, or a strupag, but would never have asked for a balgum. In fact I doubt if I ever heard the word until I married.

Many of the words I borrowed from Gaelic were derogatory, whether applied to people or to situations. Blaudaires were common in my experience, and diol-deircs. I was familiar with buisneachd—the word rather than the phenomenon. Abair e was on the tip of my tongue. I knew quite a number of people who were glugach, but I don't think I ever heard anyone described as a stammerer. I loved the glug one could get from a bottle of lemonade. Lemonade was a great luxury. It came in bottles with a spring-loaded stopper which taxed the strength of small fingers to release. Or in bottles which were sealed by a glass ball, kept in place by the pressure of the effervesence. The glass ball was even more difficult for small fingers to dislodge.

One of my favourite words was cùinn. We had to cùinn our wings and meugs when I was young. Tàmailt and tàmailteach were also in frequent use. How often have I been busach, or in the bus, with the tàmailt about something, or because I got a bioran. I would call a dwarf a druid. I thought it was the correct word for a little man. I had no idea it had anything to do with the birds that fly.

My acquaintances I might classify as spaideal, or clobhdach, or slaodach, or luideach, although luideach I would apply most naturally to something flabby, like a half-hearted handshake. Oinseach and gloichd I would use without regard to sex or gender. I never turned a somersault in my life, although I frequently made car-a-mhuiltean. But why did I call a stone an ollag? Most of my young life was spent throwing ollags at tin cans, or bottles, floating in the harbour.

I was familiar with faoileag, and knew it was the Gaelic for seagull, but I would never use it. I preferred to the onomatopoetic Stornoway slang term, gull-ag. But the sea-swallows which attacked us on the old Melbost Golf Course were never that, or terns. They were always steàrnags. Where did I get that word? None of the youngsters I golfed with were Gaelic-speakers, and we saw steàrnags nowhere else.

Our bread was often còsach or tòiseach but, while I was familiar with the word marag, it was always black (or white) puddings we spoke about. Clobht-sgurach I would apply properly to what I would more naturally call a scouring cloot, and I would apply it, derivatively, to people who lacked backbone. I knew a bròinein bochd when I saw one, although I might have applied the term to the wrong sex as well as the right one. I have heard my aunts describe someone as a gobhlan-gaoith, and fell in love with the sound of it, but I would probably have been content myself with amadan. Or amadan gòrach.

At almost every mealtime, my anxiety to know what I was getting was gently stifled with the formula "Cul a bhiogais", which, I believe, is almost as impenetrable a mystery in Gaelic as it is in English, but which I understood the significance of perfectly. Seventy years on, I use the same formula, in similar situations, with nephews even further removed from the Gaelic scene than I was.

Ablach, palag, trusdair, ceard, clo-Buckoch, peitean mor, troc, caoran, straic, all came trippingly from the tongue, as if they were English. But why did I call the tinkers jaucies? I have heard it suggested that it was a corruption of one of their common forenames—Joseph.

Gruamach, fliuch, truaghan, truas, sgrios, tuchal, bruthach, eiginneach, sgluis, sgluiseach, sgleòid, brugan, biog, 'se beagan, èisd, ma's fhior, michailmhor, spòg and spàg. All these were part of my boyhood English. In common currency, in a home where Gaelic, as such, was never used. They come welling back into my mind as I write, having lain there fallow for many years, since I set them aside in the class-room. However, dichiollach I might be in the pursuit, I doubt if I could ever recapture them all.

And some remain a mystery. Why, for instance, did I always call an old man a bru?

Even those I do recall are not really the words I knew. They sound all right, but they look all wrong. I never wrote them, or saw them written, when I used them, but I visualised them in English. I could not have spelt them in English even if I had tried, because English cannot cope with many of the Gaelic sounds, but I had a vague picture of them in my mind which was very unlike the reality.

It was a sad, benighted state to be in, in a Gaelic-speaking island. But many native Gaelic-speakers were in little better case. The schools strove to make everyone literate in English, but even fluent Gaelic-speakers would have seen their native language in print only in the Bible which they took to church, and in *Litir a Bearnaraidh* in the *Stornoway Gazette*.

But most Gaelic-speakers had the great advantage of oral bilingualism at least. An advantage the Scottish Education Department has never really accepted, or understood.

One day in the Nicolson, when a class was discussing brewing—in a geography lesson, let me hasten to add!—a Stornoway boy replied to a question with the cryptic words, "there was no cop* on it."

"No what on it?" demanded the puzzled teacher.

"No cop on it," persisted the boy, just as puzzled by the teacher's failure to understand, as the teacher was by his vocabulary.

The Gaelic-speaking members of the class had the key to the mystery. Cop is Gaelic. The English-speaking boy from Stornoway thought it was English. The English-speaking teacher from the south had never even heard the word before.

Cathie, in whose class it happened, told me the story when I fell into a similar trap myself. One day, when she was smoothing down the bed-clothes, I said, quite innocently, "There's still a lurc† in it." Not that I visualised the

*Froth
†Wrinkle

word that way. I would have spelt it with a "k", and defended with my life the proposition that it was English. It has certainly been part of my English as far back as I can recall.

Which underpins my thesis that my teachers, in the Nicolson, would have improved my English, if they had taught me Gaelic, when I asked for it.

And that seems a suitable paradox on which to pause, in this search for the identity of Lewis, which, in an earlier book, I have called Surprise Island, with some justification.

There are, however, many surprises still in store.